THE BOATOWNER'S HOW-TO GUIDES
ENGINE MAINTENANCE & REPAIR

David MacLean

TAB BOOKS
Blue Ridge Summit, Pa. 17214

FIRST EDITION

FIRST PRINTING—NOVEMBER 1977

Copyright © 1977 by TAB BOOKS

Printed in the United States
of America

Library of Congress Cataloging in Publication Data

MacLean, David, 1921-

    Engine maintenance & repair.

    (Boatowner's hot-to guides)
    Includes index.
    1. Motor-boat engines—Maintenance and repair.
    I. Title.
VM771.M3   623.87'23'4   77-21102
ISBN 0-8306-7943-X
ISBN 0-8306-6943-5 pbk.

Cover photo courtesy of Glastron, Austin TX.

To Chuck Taylor who made it happen.

CONTENTS

INTRODUCTION

In Book 1 of this series, *Hull Care and Repair*, we described our concept for a personalized Planned Preventive Maintenance program (PPM) for the small craft owner. Such a program will more than pay off in terms of increased boat usage time and at lower costs with an attendant increase in the boat's resale value. The reader should consider carefully the methods, techniques, and procedures described and adopt those suitable to his nature, his capabilities as a handyman, and his pocketbook. We shall review as many of the basic concepts as possible here.

THE ENEMIES OF BOATS

It is an understatement to say that boats operate in a hostile environment. Although the majority of registered boats in the United States are operated in the inland fresh water ponds, lakes, and rivers, far from salty seawaters, most boating publications seem to be orientated and aimed only at the salt water boatman. However, the fresh water skipper's boat faces all of the enemies of the salt water boat, less one—salt. This loss of one enemy is more than made up by the increase in another hazard—the heavy traffic conditions in restricted fresh water areas.

What we refer to as "enemies" others call "hazards." But hazard implies something that although dangerous is passive, suggesting that the hazard just sits there waiting to entrap your boat. In our terminology, the enemy is active, constantly attacking, never relenting. The skipper must constantly battle a variety of enemies, erecting new defenses and renewing them

1

often. That never-ending battle is what this book and all the others in the series is all about.

The following paragraphs are a review of the enemies of boats, the causes, effects, and some broad-brush cures.

Sunlight

Neither man, nor animals, nor plants (except for the fungi) could survive without the rays of the sun. However, for a boat the sun's high energy rays (especially those in the ultra-violet energy bands) are mostly destructive. Indiscriminantly, these rays attack paint, plastic, and gel coats of fiberglass boats. Indirectly, they might provide the extra energy required to hasten the undesirable chemical effects of the free oxygen atoms in the air and water on metal, causing rust and corrosion. It is true that except for outboard motors, most boat engines are below decks and are therefore protected from the direct effects of ultra-violet ray bombardment. Sunlight causes the dulling and chalking effect on gel coats of fiberglass boats. It causes the fading and chalking of regular paint on wood and aluminum boats.

Working with other enemies sun ruins canvas covers, unprotected wood, and nearly all forms of plastic. It is so powerful that it even causes ordinary glass to change its nature as witnessed by the color changes in glass bottles left in the sun for a period of time. Defenses against the ravages of sunlight include paint and paint renewal (preferably involving a paint containing some form of UV absorbent chemicals), keeping the boat under cover when not in use, and an awareness that sunlight is an enemy.

Air

Air carries spores of fungus and bacterial wood rot. It also carries the moisture that promotes the growth and proliferation of wood rot. A single fungus plant at work in the hull of a boat generates millions of spores, all of which can do damage. Air carries free oxygen* atoms that cause rust and corrosion of nearly all

---

*A free oxygen atom is one that has not formed a relatively harmless combination with a different atom. For example, when oxygen combines with two hydrogen atoms the result is one molecule of water. In water itself there are always a lot of oxygen atoms remaining after all the combinations with hydrogen have been made. These atoms of oxygen are said to be "free" to make other and less desirable combinations—usually with things on the boat.

metals. It is air that carries the contaminants—dust, dirt, smoke, and fumes from industrial smokestacks—that help to ruin the overall appearance of the boat. Obviously, steps must be taken to offset the effects of air.

Salt

The salt water skipper with a wood hulled boat will find that the hull that is liberally "pickled" in salt is impervious to wood rot. However, salt eats and corrodes metal surfaces. Since there is some salt—albeit in a different form—in fresh water, the fresh water skipper need not take too much comfort in the fact that the cooling water ingested by his engine will not cause the problems that it does for the salt water skipper. Much of the salt in fresh water is dissolved metallic salt that has leached into the water, either from contamination or from metal ore deposits nearby. By far the greatest salt hazard to the fresh water skipper is from the salt used on the highways to melt snow and ice. The skipper who trails his boat to and from the lake or stream over highways where the salt has been spread knows that the trailer and boat are effected by salt if the road is wet from rain even long after the winter is over. If the boat has an aluminum hull, take special precautions to rinse the boat down after any highway trip, because the type of salt used in highway safety will eat holes right through an aluminum hull.

The saltwater boatman who uses raw sea water to cool the engine can look forward to a lot of engine preventive maintenance that, in the long run, will do little good. Hot salt water flowing through the inner cooling passages of the engine block and the cast iron (usually) manifold steadily chews away at the metal. The life of an inboard engine (not designed for marine application) is far less than that of the fresh water cooled engine. The installation of a fresh water cooling system using a heat exchanger between the engine coolant and raw sea water will pay off in longer engine life but only on relatively new engines.

The ubiquitous outboard is designed and constructed of metals and materials that are, for the most part, resistant to salt water. Engines, including outboards, must be thoroughly flushed with fresh water before they are stored at the end of the boating season. If a flushing and metal preserving compound can be added during the flushing process, so much the better.

Galvanic Action

While boats in fresh water are nearly immune from this mysterious and galling enemy, salt water skippers must constantly guard against its insidious attacks. Problems stemming from galvanic action appear to be on the increase and everything from poor quality zinc sacrificial anodes to changes in the earth's magnetic fields has been blamed. This enemy works on underwater portions of the boat where the results cannot be easily observed by even the most conscientious of skippers. Regular underwater inspection of *all* metal fittings is an essential part of any salt water PPM program. The galvanic action process and what can be done to protect the boat against it will be discussed at length in the following chapters.

Wood Rot

Wherever there is fresh water and wood there is the possibility of wood rot because the spores and bacteria that cause wet and dry wood rot are transported by air and fresh water. A carelessly left pile of wood scraps in a boat yard can infect every boat within hundreds of yards, and an infected boat will start rot in other boats. Wood rot is a boat's social disease. Even fiberglass boats have wood fittings that are susceptible to wood rot. It is to our advantage that wood rot smells bad and can be located by searching the boat from stem to stern with a sharp-pointed tool. The defenses against this enemy of boats are discussed and described in *Small Craft Preventive Maintenance*.

Plants and Animals

To date, over 1900 plants and animals have been identified as threats to a boat. For the fresh water skipper these are not as great a problem as for the skipper of a salt water craft. Still there are a few plants and some animals present in fresh water that can cause trouble. To combat these problems, correct application and maintenance of the proper form of anti-fouling paint is a large part of any good PPM program.

Man

You might think it extreme that man is considered an active enemy of boats. If that is true, look at it this way. Is not man the direct cause of boat damage requiring corrective maintenance? Does he not often neglect his duties and responsibilities in regard to proper and timely preventive maintenance, thus causing needless wear and tear on his boat? And does he not stubbornly fail to learn and practice the safe way to operate and maintain a boat, thus causing expensive and often needless corrective maintenance? The prosecution rests!

ENEMIES OF ENGINES

To the preceding list of enemies may be added several more that are more specifically the enemies of engines, no matter where the boat is operated. Nowhere else does Murphy's immutable law apply more than to boats. To paraphrase Murphy's Law, whatever might go wrong in or on a small boat, will go wrong! Small craft engines, inboard or outboard, are subjected to corrosion, galvanic action, and man. In addition there is heat, vibration, mechanical stress, and friction.

One of the most difficult concepts for any small craft owner to grasp is the normal stress under which an engine operates in a boat. The boat engine, unlike the car engine, labors all the time it is in gear and the propeller or drive unit is engaged. By contrast, the car even though in gear coasts much of the time with very little stress on the engine. On the other hand, the boat engine is going up hill—virtually climbing a mountain—all the time it is in gear. This is why automotive engine conversions are less than totally satisfactory and why the outboard engine itself is a marvel of mechanical engineering. For the same reason, the diesel engine is fast becoming the small craft engine of tomorrow for it must be extra rugged even when used in a motor vehicle.

PPM: THE CONCEPT AND PROCEDURES

The intention of this book, and the others of this series, is to describe the enemies of boats and what can be done to offset their effects by PLANNED PREVENTIVE MAINTENANCE. In the following paragraphs is a brief review of the methods, techniques, and procedures that make up an effective PPM program.

The basic concept in PPM for small craft stems from the idea, supported by all kinds of statistics, that *preventive* maintenance is ten times less expensive and hundreds of times less time consuming than *corrective* maintenance. Preventive maintenance is also much easier to accomplish without highly skilled technical help. For example, it would be difficult to find anyone who could not teach himself to use a grease gun and a lubrication chart on his outdrive or the lower unit of his outboard engine. Yet, how would this same person fare if he had to replace and rebuild the gear mechanisms of the lower units because of lubrication failure?

We have never known a skipper to argue against the PPM concept, yet it is difficult to find many skippers who apply the concept in a practical manner. Boats that look and behave beautifully at all times are often professionally maintained, either by a hired crew or by a yacht yard. The expensive services of professionals are not within the means of the average small craft skipper. The lack of application of preventive maintenance programs in small craft stems from two main sources. First, most skippers do not know how to plan. Second, preventive maintenance involves a lot of just plain drudgery. We can do something about the former, but not too much about the latter. A PPM program is a three-step process. First, the craft is inspected and data gathered. Second, the gathered data is analyzed to determine a system of needs and the resources to meet them. Third, a plan is formulated based upon the accumulated "hard" data—that is, *facts* not opinions.

Inspection and Data Gathering

"Inspect—don't expect!" is sensible advice with which to begin a maintenance planning program. Start with a methodical inspection of the propulsion system. Examine carefully each of the individual subsystems of the propulsion system before going on to the next subsystem. (The subsystems of engine-powered small craft are discussed in Chapter 1.)

Make up and use check-off lists so that no element of the engine's subsystem will escape investigation. During the inspection take notes so that you'll not forget what you have found.

For the inspection, one of the most valuable tools available is the owner's manual. It was written by the people who built the engine and it is reasonable to expect that they know how to make it go.

Perhaps of even greater value, although somewhat more difficult to use, is the engine shop manual that can be purchased from the engine maker or dealer. Keep in mind, however, that this manual is written for the factory trained mechanic working in an extensively equipped shop with all the special tools, jigs and fixtures that this kind of manual will often refer to or show in illustrations. Yet when the trade jargon and elaborate technical language is stripped away, you will find enough basic information to enable you to keep your engine going without resorting to the high-priced professional mechanic. Such manuals can serve as guides to help you compose good, solid, check-off lists that will aid you in making a thorough inspection of the engine subsystems in the shortest possible time. We can generalize on method and technique but needless to say, we cannot cover every single type of engine in this limited space. Therefore, we suggest that you refer to the manual pertaining to your particular engine.

Analysis and Planning

Once the inspection of the engine has been completed and all of the factual data gathered, digest what you have seen and begin a first rough draft of the preventive maintenance plan. First, list all the things to be done, making note of the tools, materials, and instruments that will be required and where they can be obtained. Separate all the routine maintenance tasks that you know you can do—either because you have done them before or because they are simple tasks. Next, list all tasks involving alignment and adjustments. Using the shop manual, try to determine and (for the moment) mentally list the required steps and necessary special tools and instruments. Do not make any decisions yet.

Formulating Your Plan and Carrying It Out

Once you have listed and inspected each of the engine subsystems, listed and analyzed all of the preventive (and corrective) maintenance tasks required in each one, analyzed the work required and the tools, materials, and instruments needed, then and only then can you make any kind of rational decisions as to who will do the work. The greatest danger by far is the automatic assumption by the average skipper that he can't do a job that appears to involve complex adjustment but that in fact may be quite easy.

If all of this seems to add to the toil and responsibility of owning a boat, then consider the advantages and benefits of PPM planning:

1. PPM will lower your maintenance costs.
2. PPM will shorten the time required for maintenance.

3.   PPM will eliminate all but the kind of catastrophic failure
      that *nothing* could prevent.

4.   PPM, faithfully carried out, cannot help but enhance the
      resale value of any boat.

5.   A PPM boat is a safer boat, a better running boat, a better
      looking boat.

To carry out your PPM program you will of course need various tools, instruments, materials, and supplies. Using the suggestions in this book, you should be able to assemble a good assortment of tools suitable to your capabilities, pocketbook, and maintenance program. Do not go overboard on tools—never have they been so expensive. If you acquire a good basic set of tools, most of the special tools required can be borrowed or rented—or put them on your Christmas, Father's Day, and birthday lists. Watch for sales in the local hardware and department stores. Look for good used tools at yard and garage sales, but get there early as tools go first. Consider also purchasing several test and alignment instruments. In the past, most of these would have been considered beyond the reach and skill level of the average skipper of today, but this is no longer true. Because these instruments are no longer designed exclusively for the professional, the manufacturer is able to cut corners, mostly in the ruggedness of the instruments, which in no way detracts from their usefulness on an intermittent basis. While they might not last a week in the professional's shop, they will last for years in the PPM skipper's shoreside tool locker. Pricewise, they will pay for themselves the first few times they are used and, as an added advantage, they can be used to keep the family car and other vehicles in top condition.

We will also tell you about a number of "tricks of the trade" that we have discovered over the years, which are all that separate the professional from the amateur in many cases. Finally, we will have a lot to say about one of the most neglected areas of maintenance—small craft documentation.

1
MARINE ENGINES, A SYSTEM

In *Hull Care and Repair* we considered and dealt with a small craft as a system composed of a number of subsystems. The same concept applies to the propulsion system of a boat with an internal combustion engine. The propulsion system of a sailboat (sails, masts, spars, rigging, etc.) generally requires only corrective maintenance. Naturally, some preventive maintenance must be done, but once installed and in regular use there is little to be done (in a preventive sense) to the windjammer's propulsion system. The special problems of maintaining sailboats are treated in another book in this series.

Illustrated here, in diagrammatic form, are the elements comprising the subsystems in a mechanical propulsion system of a small craft. The diagram is applicable to two-cycle (outboard engines), four-cycle (inboard or the so-called inboard/outboard engines), and, by the deletion of the ignition system, to diesel engines. Note that the diagram lists the major components of each of the various subsystems of an engine. We will discuss each of these major component's "soft spots", a term used by industrial designers and engineers.

Many skippers become disillusioned about the maintainability of inboard engines installed in small cramped quarters where it is impossible to carry out the most simple maintenance with any comfort or convenience. One of the more crucial preventive maintenance requirements of inboard four-cycle engines is periodic changing of lubrication oil after a certain number of use-hours on the engine. The engine oil drain plug, placed for the convenience of automotive installations, usually ends up, in a boat, in an inaccessible location. There is often no

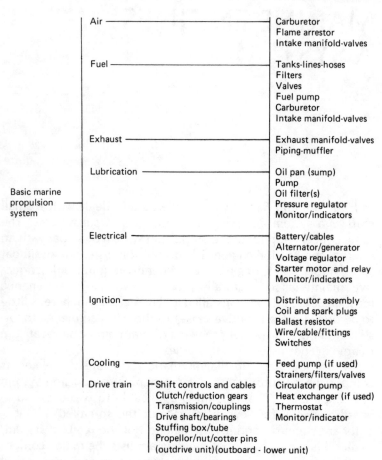

Fig. 1.1   The systems comprising a small craft engine.

room to get a container into the space under the engine to drain the oil into, and when there is space you may find that when the pan is filled with oil there is no way to get it out of the bilge without spilling it, thereby causing a fire hazard and assuring a filthy greasy bilge.

Only in the last few years have marine engine assemblers included threaded fittings at the end of the dip stick tubes to facilitate the connection of an expensive oil draining pump which you must buy, borrow, or rent. Later in this chapter you will find some suggested methods of draining engine oil that do not require expensive pumps or leave an impossible mess in the boat.

THE AIR SUBSYSTEM

Included in the air system of an internal combustion engine (marine) are such elements as the carburetor, the backfire flame arrester (required by Federal regulation on all inboard gasoline fuel engines), intake manifolds, and intake valves. The maintenance soft spots in this subsystem include the carburetor and the backfire flame arrester.

Modern *carburetors* are extremely complex devices requiring a small but reliable amount of preventive maintenance. Troubles in this area stem from the formation of undesirable sticky, shellac-like substances from the gasoline and ordinary dirt and dust from the air rushing into the intake throat of the carburetor. These substances often cause sticking or malfunctioning in the automatic choke systems, throttle plates, float mechanisms, and both choke and throttle linkages. Fortunately for us there are a number of chemical products available (usually in spray form) that when applied to and around the carburetor will dissolve the unwanted formations so they can be easily flushed away. Other chemicals can be poured directly into the carburetor air intake of a running engine to free up sticking choke and throttle plates. Perhaps easiest and best of all, some of these preparations may be added directly to the fuel tanks where they flow right along with the fuel, cleaning and unsticking the whole system. Sticking problems are often more acute in outboard engines where lubrication oil is mixed in the fuel before it reaches the carburetor. It is important not to allow such a mixture to set in tanks, fuel pumps, lines, and carburetors as it will form a shellac-like substance that will foul up the whole fuel system.

Although there are a number of adjustments on the modern carburetor, they rarely require attention unless there has been a radical change in either the fuel or air inputs. Except for the idle speed adjust and the idle mixture adjust (described in later chapters), all of these adjustments should be left to the professional factory-trained mechanic.

Fig. 1.2   Typical backfire flame arrester found on inboard gasoline engines.

The *backfire flame arrester* may seem to be little more than some sort of air filter placed on top of the carburetor. However, its important purpose is to prevent any open flame from an engine backfire (through the carburetor) from entering the open engine compartment where it might ignite gasoline vapors. A series of one-way baffles arranged around the perimeter of the unit accomplishes this purpose with reasonable efficiency. Unfortunately, air and oily fumes being fed from the valve case covers (on newer engines) cause the collection of greasy black dirt on the outside of the fins and baffles and, if not periodically cleaned off, the flame arrester will act as an unwanted choke on the engine. The cleaning of the flame arrester must be high on your list of preventive maintenance tasks.

In some of the older marine engine installations side-mounted, updraft carburetors are used. In addition to a backfire flame arrester, a drip pan to catch gasoline running out of the carburetor must be included, by law, in the installation. Other than cleaning—which is anything but routine—the backfire flame arresters do not cause trouble.

The *intake manifold*, which may also be regarded as part of the fuel system, ordinarily is not an automotive maintenance soft spot. However, due to the added stresses imposed by operation in the marine environment, it should be inspected from time to time for cracks and gasket leaks, and a program of rust and corrosion prevention should be routinely carried out.

Fig. 1.3   Backfire flame arrester required on side or up draft carburetors of an inboard marine gasoline engine.

THE FUEL SUBSYSTEM

In the fuel system there are a number of small but important soft spots. *Fuel tanks* themselves are not as much a problem as the fluid they contain. One of the most persistent problems is water in the fuel. If the boat is stored during the off season with partly filled fuel tanks, any water accumulation inside the tank may cause severe problems later. Depending on the type of tank holding the fuel, water might cause rust and corrosion inside the tank. Flakes of rusted metal slough off the tank and find their way into the fuel system, to clog filters and disable pumps and carburetors. A regular program of fuel treatment with fuel additives is a must in a PPM program. Certain forms of alcohol readily mix with water, and the resultant mixture will combine with gasoline and be consumed in the engine. These chemical additives, poured into the tank before off-season storage, will effectively prevent most of the problems. The most dangerous problem associated with fuel tanks in the past was pin-hole leaks caused by rust and corrosion. Consequently the Coast Guard has ordered that the use of metals subject to this problem be discontinued. A periodic inspection of your fuel tank installation must be included in the PPM program, for there is much to look for here and *prevention* is the *only* thing that works.

Fuel filters on a marine engine are not a luxury but an absolute necessity. A good installation will include at least two filters—one in the fuel line between the tank and the fuel pump and a second on the pump itself. Some of the new engines include a replaceable paper filter right where the fuel line from the pump enters the carburetor. The PPM program includes the periodic inspection of the filters, the replacement of disposable cartridges and the backflushing and cleaning of the permanent type of filter elements. In addition, anything that the filter has trapped must be studied to determine if anything undesirable is going on in the fuel system. Your PPM program must include a periodic inspection of all fuel lines, valves, and hose clamps for tightness and no-leak integrity. If you find any of the ring clip type of hose clamps, remove and discard them immediately. Substitute high quality stainless steel screw type hose clamps and stop worrying about cut and leaking rubber fuel lines.

The *fuel pump*, when it is considered what it does and how, is not a soft spot nor can we rightfully include it in a PPM program other than to recommend that the fuel pump be periodically inspected with the rest of the fuel system. Modern automotive fuel pumps, for the most part, are sealed units and cannot be repaired or rebuilt. For this reason a spare pump should be carried in the boat box of the PPM skipper. Many of the new pumps have an external glass sight bowl (not an integral part of the pump, which is illegal by federal regulation) to indicate, by the presence of gasoline in the bowl, that the pump has failed and a new pump must be installed immediately. The pump has a double diaphragm and will continue to feed fuel to the engine but should be replaced at the earliest moment. Formerly the glass sight bowl at the base of automotive type fuel pumps was also a part of a filter. For this reason the automotive type of fuel pump must not be used on a boat unless the filter bowl is changed to a metal bowl.

The fuel system shares the carburetor, the intake manifold, and the intake valves with the air system, as previously discussed. Other than what already has been described, routine careful inspection, faithfully and periodically practiced, is the only preventive maintenance that applies to these elements.

THE EXHAUST SUBSYSTEM

Like the automotive exhaust system, the marine engine's *exhaust system* is a major soft spot for maintenance. When you consider the stresses that the marine engine's exhaust manifold is subjected to, it is a miracle that it lasts as long as it does. If

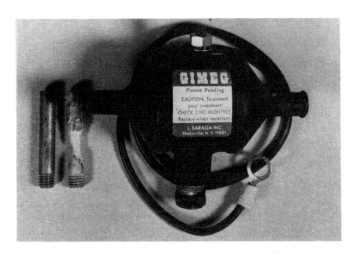

Fig. 1.4 The L. Saraga Inc. "GIMEG" designed to protect inboard engines and manifolds from the ravages of galvanic action, is shown here with spare zinc.

the engine uses a raw water cooling system and the raw water is salt, this is even more of a miracle. *Hot* salt water has an extreme effect on most metals. Many different systems and types of metals have been developed in an effort to extend the life of the average exhaust manifold on a marine engine. Stainless steel is effective when the steel is galvanically insulated from the cast iron or aluminum engine block.

The cast iron exhaust manifold is still in use and the PPM skipper will be wise to include it in his PPM program. If he needs further motivation, let him take note of the replacement costs for a new manifold. Today, several things can be done to extend the life of a cast iron exhaust manifold. There are a few firms that will coat the inside of the manifold with ceramic layers, especially in the water passages.

Many skippers with salt water cooling do not know that the inside of the manifold is heavily subjected to galvanic action, which effectively destroys the manifold. A device called the GIMEG can be installed in the raw water cooling line. It has replaceable zinc anodes that screw into a base plug and make anode changing a snap. On a new (and perhaps even an old) engine, these little gadgets should pay for themselves in terms of extended manifold and engine life. The skipper with a raw salt water cooling system in his new boat should carefully consider the economics of installing one of the new closed-loop fresh water cooling systems. Those fortunate skippers who operate a boat where the float water is fresh will not have this problem to face.

Exhaust manifolds are subject not only to rust, corrosion, and galvanic action, but in addition face the problems of extreme ranges of heat. Impurities in the cooling water, such as salt, silt, or oily carbon and sulfur wastes from the engine, may be precipitated out of the water because of the extreme heat and cake the insides of the water passages. These undesirable coatings restrict the flow of cooling water, cause turbulence in the flow and, as a result, cause hot spots to develop and generate further problems. Since most manifolds, though simple to replace, are still made of cast iron and are very expensive, a PPM program will really pay off.

In nearly all inboards the hot exhaust gases and near boiling hot water, having passed through the exhaust manifolds, pass through some sort of *piping* before being discharged through the stern or transom. This piping is subjected to the same stresses as the manifolds but often must also endure vibration. The more piping, the more stress from vibration is involved. Problems arise with pipe hangers, supports, clamps and other fittings, which must be carefully and systematically inspected in anticipation of problems. Fortunately, skippers with outboard engines can be less concerned about their exhaust systems because the designers have considered the problems and, for the most part, have solved them. Still, the outboard engine needs periodic flushing in fresh water before post-season layup. If this is done professionally in an engine shop, preserving chemicals will often be added to the flushing water to further inhibit the formation of corrosion and rust.

Any small craft skipper fortunate enough to possess a diesel engine should keep in mind that the manifolds of even this engine are subjected to all of the foregoing problems. In addition, he must be aware that formation of sulphuric acid in the exhaust is a further problem. The sulphur content in the fuel varies from one load of fuel to another and, generally speaking, is not something the skipper can control. Sulphur present in varying degrees is a factor contributing to shortening the life of the diesel exhaust manifold.

At the end of this chapter we have included a complete exhaust manifold PPM program which you can do yourself and which will pay off in the extended life of these very expensive parts.

THE LUBRICATION SUBSYSTEM

The lubrication subsystem is one of the few areas of the engine that does not cause the *average* skipper recurrent problems. Perhaps it is because the oil itself protects the system to a large extent. In any case, a simple but important PPM program here will include the *routine* changing of the oil and oil filter at the *end* of the boating season. Or, if you are one of those fortunate skippers who enjoys a long semi-tropical boating period, then the oil and filter should be changed when the boat is hauled for its annual overhaul. In any case, the recommendations in the owner's manual should be followed.

Usually the owner's manual uses *engine operating hours* as a guideline—the only practical way of evaluating when the engine is due for various maintenance activities. For this reason, you should keep a record of the total time that the engine is in actual use. The easiest way, of course, is to have installed an elapsed time meter, which usually is connected to the ignition switch so that the meter records only when the switch is on. Such a meter may be expensive but it will more than pay for itself. Otherwise, use the inexpensive method of keeping an accurate and faithful engine log. The problem with this method is that self-discipline is required to enter faithfully every use time on the engine.

An accurate engine log has many uses other than recording in-use hours. It can be PPM notes and information, problems encountered and how they were solved, all cost data (perhaps for tax purposes), where parts and materials were produced and how they stood up, etc.

Still another device for keeping track of engine use time is a 12-volt electric clock from an automotive junk yard. The clock can be installed with its electric leads connected across the ignition switch so that the clock only runs when the engine is running. The obvious drawback is that such a clock will only record twelve hours before it starts over again. Thus, each twelve-hour cycle must be recorded if the system is to be of any use.

The inboard engine *oil lubrication pump* and *pressure regulating bypass* valve are, in almost all cases, buried in the engine and are therefore inaccessible to inspection except with some form of instrumentation. However, these parts can fail. Immediately shut down the engine where there is any indication, either by meter, light, or audio alarm, that there has been a radical drop in lubricating oil pressure to the engine. At the beginning of the boating season the engine oil pan (sump) should be inspected using a mirror and a flashlight to search for leaks around the pan's retaining bolts and gaskets. Check each bolt for tightness using a socket wrench and remembering that you are looking at the bolt upside down. The oil drain plug at the bottom of the oil pan should also be checked for tightness.

On most modern marine engines an electrically operated pressure switch monitors the engine oil pressure. The switch is *normally* closed—that is, when there is *no* pressure, the switch will activate a lamp at the operating position. When engine oil pressure builds up to the operating level (almost immediately during the starting cycle), the pressure will cause the switch to open and the oil pressure warning light to go out. One advantage of this system is that a small very inexpensive 12-volt buzzer can be connected directly across the lamp terminals to give the skipper an audio warning of loss of oil pressure even if his attention is elsewhere when the lamp comes on.

A second and more traditional monitoring method utilizes a thin small metal tube to conduct the oil sample to an appropriate instrument at the operating panel. Unfortunately, at least in the marine environment, these small tubes are subjected to corrosion and vibration that may cause them to rupture and spray black oil all over. (In the event of a rupture, pinch the tube closed with pliers until you can replace it.)

In yet another system the sender is a pressure-varied resistor which converts oil pressure in the engine to equivalent amounts of resistance to electric current which is transmitted to a display instrument. The electric current flows through an electric meter which is calibrated and registered in oil pounds of pressure. Once you have assured yourself that the monitoring system is accurate, there is little maintenance you can do other than remove and replace senders, wire or tubes, and meters and lamps.

THE ELECTRICAL SUBSYSTEM

The Battery

In its yearly statistical reports the Coast Guard states that the main cause of calls for assistance is a dead or run-down *battery*.

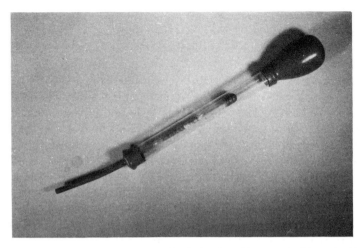

Fig. 1.5   Best for evaluating the worth of a lead acid battery, is this typical hydrometer.

While these statistics are not further broken down to pinpoint the primary cause of battery failure, it is generally agreed to be failure on the part of the operating skipper to provide the minimum of preventive maintenance care to the battery. A modern marine engine, be it inboard or outboard, of any appreciable horsepower and high compression ratios, cannot be started manually. The lead-acid battery should be thought of as a chemical engine—that is, it converts chemical energy to electrical energy. Even when the environment it operates in is benign, the normal chemical activity of the battery can cause trouble. In a marine environment, the problems multiply. Because of this and because the battery is so crucial to the operation of a small craft, a preventive maintenance program faithfully carried out is the only way to avoid serious problems.

Check the battery cable terminals by removing the cables. The white powdery crystals that form on these terminals are highly resistant to the flow of electric current, and a low-voltage system (such as a lead-acid battery) cannot endure the smallest voltage drop. Remove the battery and inspect the electrolyte level (liquid). It must never be too low to cover the tops of the battery plates visible under the filler vent caps. Make absolutely sure that the vent holes that allow battery gas to escape during charge periods are free from dirt and plugging. Obtain and learn to use a battery hydrometer (they are inexpensive) to periodically measure each cell's specific gravity and record it in the engine log. Any variation between cells predicts the imminent demise of the battery and warns you in advance to replace it. (A small floating colored ball type of hydrometer can be stored right on the top of the battery.)

Keep the top of the battery clean of oily residue from engine vapor and the oxides that form from the battery action itself. Rinse battery case with baking soda and clean water. Distilled water from any drug store is best for a lead-acid battery. Local tap water usually contains a lot of iron as well as other undesirable chemicals which will surely shorten the life of the battery. Inspect and clean *both* ends of *both* battery cables. Once clean, a coating of Vaseline will keep voltage-eating oxides off the surface of the terminals.

Inspect the condition of the *alternator-generator* drive belt and test the degree of tension. Firm pressure from the thumb should depress the belt about one-half inch. If the belt is too loose, the alternator-generator might not charge the battery. Too tight a belt will quickly take out the machine's pulley bearing, which usually means that the entire device must be replaced. Inspect the connections on the back of the alternator-generator for cleanliness and tightness. Because they are often covered with rubber boots they may be neglected.

Electric starter motors, starting solenoids, and alternator-generators will be covered in detail as to both preventive and corrective maintenance in *Small Craft Electrical Maintenance*. On most modern engines, both inboard and outboard, the voltage regulators are of the solid state variety in which the complex relays have been replaced by transistors and diodes as sensing and control devices. As a rule these cannot be serviced and the entire sealed and potted unit must be replaced. However, the wires and terminals can be inspected and kept clean, which will, for the most part, prevent a lot of problems. The ammeters, fuses, and all cable and wire both at the engine and at the operator's position should be inspected on a periodic basis for the usual connection tightness and cleanliness of the terminals and terminal lugs.

The Ignition System

If there is a super soft spot in any marine engine, it is the *ignition system* which is why we are treating it separately. PPM will really pay off in terms of better overall performance. Failure in a marine engine ignition system follows a fairly consistent pattern. Most failures are preventable, and fortunately *any* skipper can do most or all of the preventive maintenance. The prime trouble-makers are distributor caps and rotors, point sets, spark plugs, and spark plug wires. Since marine engines are not normally subjected to the stop and go of road traffic, most of them do not include the troublesome automatic vacuum advance system. The mechanical advance weights in the distributor are adequate for the job. Some marine engines that have been directly converted from automotive sources still retain the vacuum advance, which is, for all practical purposes, useless.

Marine engines today require substantially increased voltage to fire the spark plugs. The increase in firing voltage, however, is often not matched by a lasting increase in the insulation resistance in distributor caps and ignition harness. Also, any water vapor in the air fed to the engine is attracted to the ignition system by the high voltages. As a result, all low-and high-voltage wiring, all terminals, both studs and lugs, all metal cases, such as coils, distributor bodies, and ballast resistors, are apt to rust and corrode. As rust and corrosion build up in the overall circuit, electric current is inhibited and the system soon becomes marginal. The smallest decrease in the voltage available and the system fails. The skipper with a PPM program, who understands the cause of this failure, assumes these components *will* fail and takes simple precautionary steps.

A good PPM program will include a complete examination of the ignition system at the beginning of every season (detailed in a later chapter) and also includes a periodic inspection program during the boating season.

THE COOLING SYSTEM

In an automobile the *cooling system* (the liquid part, at least) can be minimal and still perform adequately. This is due primarily to the abundance of cooling air flowing over and around the automobile's engine in addition to the air that is cooling the radiator. By contrast, the marine engine, buried in the bilges if an inboard, or covered with a spray protecting shroud if an outboard, receives barely enough air to feed the carburetor and very little to spare for cooling the engine. The cooling burden is placed totally on the liquid cooling system, whatever type it might be. The PPM skipper knows that his marine engine's system is intolerant of any partial performance by *any* component of that system. By far the weakest point in any marine cooling system has to be the pump(s). Extremely reliable pumps have been designed, built, and installed in small craft, but other factors can cause such pumps to *appear* to fail. For example, a boat travelling along at 3000 RPM's can take into its pump a discarded plastic sandwich bag. At that speed, a rubber impeller type pump instantly eats its own innards and the engine rapidly overheats due to the lack of circulating cooling water. If the situation is allowed to persist, the engine may seize up tight. Yet, as it can be seen, the trouble was not directly caused by pump failure.

When the boat is stored ashore during the off season the pump impeller (if it is the rubber type) can take a set—because it is held in one position for weeks on end. The impeller assumes the shape of that position and no longer pumps an adequate amount of feed water to the engine circulating pump. Coolant hoses, hose clamps, and, as we have already mentioned, manifolds are subjected to extreme heat, vibration, rust and corrosion. The caking of deposits from impurities in the cooling water that restrict the needed volume of cooling water flow are yet another problem to contend with.

All marine engines, inboards and outboards, use thermostats of various types to control and regulate the flow of cooling water circulating within the engine. Because of the limitations already cited, these devices must perform almost perfectly and are, therefore, difficult to design and construct. For the PPM skipper, it is a simple matter to remove and test the thermostat before the season begins and thus better assure the adequate performance of the engine operating temperature control device for the season.

If you have an inboard engine with a circulating pump in addition to the raw water feed pump, you can expect to have trouble with bearings not designed for marine work. The same is true of the metal impellers and the removable back plates. No small part of the problem with these all-metallic pumps is the presence of galvanic action because, as a rule, these pumps were designed for automotive use and incorporate several different metals. An automotive pump, which often lasts the life of the car, modified for marine application, will often fail and require complete replacement at substantial expense.

Most small craft marine engines, either inboard or outboard, indicate an overtemperature condition in the engine by a

red lamp mounted at the operator's position. The lamp is activated when a heat-controlled switch closes. This switch is usually installed in the engine at a strategic location in the cooling
system, often near the thermostat itself, and will quickly pick up
any radical increase in the heat of the cooling water temperature. It is a bimetallic switch constructed of two metals with
radically different coefficients of expansion. These metals are
bonded together in such a way that when sufficient heat is applied, one of the metals will bend and touch the other which, in
turn, completes an electrical circuit and lights the lamp. A certain degree of "detent" is built into these switches, so that the
switch might close (for example) at 220° but would not open
again until the temperature dropped to 190°. These switches
and the associated electrical system persist in causing faulty indications and must be periodically tested in a pan of water. The
simple but effective procedures for testing these devices are included in the next section of this chapter.

THE DRIVE TRAIN

In the drive train are included such elements as shift controls,
cables, and associated safety micro-switches. The main parts of
the drive train include clutches, reduction gears, shaft couplings (a major soft spot), stuffing boxes, drive shafts, struts and
propellers, propeller retaining nuts and safety cotter pins. In the
outboard and the drive unit of the inboard/outboard (I/O) most
of these elements are present but in different form and design.
The drive train of an I/O is subjected to the added strain of a
drive shaft that must make two 90-degree changes in direction,
which means extra gears, bearings, and/or universal joints that
require most careful periodic preventive maintenance—mostly
lubrication.

When a small craft is stored ashore on a cradle or trailer
during the off season, a totally different stress is placed on the
hull compared with the stresses afloat. If the boat is a regular inboard, it may be better to disconnect the drive shaft at its coupling to the transmission so that the set of the hull, while on land,
will not affect the alignment of the drive shaft and coupling.
After launching and soaking the hull, the drive shaft and coupling can be reconnected using a feeler gauge to make sure there
has been no change in shaft alignment. This is a problem unique
to inboard craft.

While not directly associated with the drive train, the sacrificial zinc anodes are, for the most part, designed to protect the drive train elements from attack by galvanic action. They must therefore be carefully maintained. Check their condition, and the condition of the attaching nuts and bolts, to make sure they are doing what they are designed to do.

2
SMALL CRAFT
"TRICKS OF THE TRADE"

In a lifetime of association with small craft, I have managed to acquire a number of the so-called tricks of the trade, some of which follow. These have been selected on the basis of their usefulness, ease of application, and general low cost.

THE MAGNETIZED DIP STICK

Let us consider Murphy's Law as it applies to objects dropped in a small craft. Whatever can be dropped in a boat will be—and it will most likely be a small part crucial to the boat's operation, which will roll into the darkest most inaccessible part of the bilge, and be almost impossible to pick up if it is ever located. To contend with this, you can magnetize the engine's dip stick by wrapping several turns of scrap wire around its end, (The number of turns is not important, but the more the better.) Hold the turns in place with a bit of masking tape and loosely connect one end of the coil of wire to the negative terminal of any lead-acid battery (making absolutely sure there are no gasoline fumes present). Then, holding the other end of the coil by the insulation, "flash" the bare end of the coil wire on the positive battery terminal. (Brush it across the terminal several times.) This will cause a dramatic but harmless spark. Don't hold the wire to the terminal since it is virtually a dead short across the battery and will burn up the wire in short order. This treatment will make the hard steel end of the dip stick a permanent magnet. The coil of scrap wire is removed and returned to the "possibles box" for future use. The magnetized dip stick now has a number of uses other than the simple measurement of oil level in the oil sump

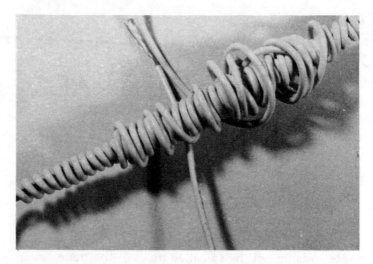

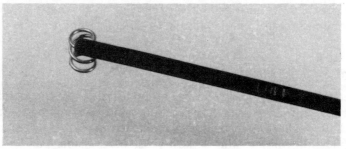

Fig. 2.1   Using the principles of electro-magnetism makes the end of the engine oil dip stick a permanent magnet.

of the engine. It can be used to retrieve small metal parts that have fallen into otherwise inaccessible places in the bilge. When stored in its normal position in the oil sump it will attract and hold any bits of metal that might find their way into the oil supply.

THE CLOTHESPIN HIGH VOLTAGE TESTER

From time to time it is necessary to determine where the loss of an ignition voltage is occurring. When the voltage in question is associated with the output of the ignition coil or when a spark plug wire is suspect, the usual procedure is to remove the wire (in the case of the distributor coil wire) and hold it close to, but

Fig. 2.2   Using the common clothes pin to test for spark.

not touching, the metal of the engine. Since there is often as much as 14,000 volts present (more if the system is electronic), there is danger of an unpleasant (but not lethal) shock. To avoid this you can wrap the wire where you intend to hold it in several layers of *dry* paper or cloth; you can buy an expensive pair of insulated pliers just for this task; or you can use a spring type wooden clothespin. The wooden clothespin is an excellent insulator and may be used to hold the coil or plug wires to test for spark without the danger of inducing a shock. The coil wire is removed from the distributor, held by the clothespin close to a metal ground on the engine as the engine is cranked with the ignition key ON. If all is well, a bright blue spark will jump from the metal end of the coil wire to the engine block. Much the same procedure is used to check single spark plug wires, although it may be necessary to insert something like an old shear pin in the end of the rubber plug boot in order to get a spark out of it.

A LOW COST EMERGENCY HOSE REPAIR KIT

Modern marine engines—even outboards—require an amazing number and variety of rubber hoses to convey various liquids from one point to another. Almost any one of these hoses, if it fails for any reason, can disable the engine. There are two alternative provisions against the possible failure of an engine hose.

Fig. 2.3   The handy (and cheap) coolant hose emergency repair kit.

One alternative, of course, is to purchase, pre-cut, and store at least one spare for every hose on the engine. A far simpler, and much less expensive, second alternative has the added advantage of not requiring much on-board storage space. The photograph shows our suggestion for an emergency repair kit for rubber hoses that will provide coverage for almost any hose aboard. The couplings shown are poly-vinyl-chloride (PVC) fittings that are readily available in most hardware stores and, as can be seen, come in many sizes that will fit the inside diameter (ID) of all or most of the engine's hoses.

When a hose fails it is usually because of a crack or a bubble in the wall of the hose which, sooner or later, breaks. To repair the damaged hose, cut out the damaged section. This leaves a gap in the hose, of course, but the gap is easily filled by selecting the appropriate size (inside diameter) of PVC hose coupling and sliding a stainless steel hose clamp onto each end of the cut hose, inserting the hose coupling into the ends of the cut hose and tightening the hose clamps over the ends of the cut hose and the PVC couplings. If the damage is at the end of the hose, it can be cut and the remaining length of hose can be extended with the PVC coupler. The PVC couplings cost pennies and the stainless steel screw-type clamps, while not cheap, are extensively adjustable so that only a few are needed to make up a kit.

METHODS AND TECHNIQUES FOR LOOSENING RUSTED OR CORRODED MARINE FASTENERS

Often one of the most frustrating tasks facing the PPM skipper is the disassembly of some unit on the marine engine which necessitates breaking loose a nut, bolt, or screw that has "seized" up. Engine fasteners are subjected to extremes of heat and the usual effects of rust and corrosion which create a bond between the male threads of the fastener and the female threads of the holding element. The breaking of this bond can be difficult. Brute strength rarely works except to generate substantially worse problems in terms of sheared off bolts and screws. Keep in mind that the immediate objective is to break the seal formed between the threads of the fastener and the part held. To this end, apply guile, not force. There are several alternative methods and techniques available, and when one won't work or does not suit the situation, the chances are that another one will.

Metal Nuts

This method of loosening metal nuts is based upon the "shock" or "impact" wrench techniques. Shock or impact wrenches are power-driven either by air or electric motor and provide torque or twisting action to the nut socket by means of thousands of short-duration blows to the shaft of the tool. The vibration and extreme torque quickly backs out the most stubborn wheel fastener. Also available is a similar tool, called a *hand impact wrench*, that is operated by hand using a heavy machinist's hammer. Like the impact wrench, there are available a number of different heads such as sockets and screwdriver blades for various type of screws. If you can't borrow or rent one, these tools can be found in automotive supply stores and are listed in the Sears Roebuck catalog for under $12.

The use of yet another special tool—the universal nut cracker—is probably the fastest and easiest way to release a seized nut. The tool, which is no more than a nut cracker, is fitted over the stubborn nut. A threaded shaft is turned with a wrench, forcing a hardened blade to cut into the body of the nut and easily break it loose from its parent stud or bolt. Although the nut is destroyed in the process, it can be replaced easily and inexpensively. This tool can also be found in automotive supply stores and is listed in the Sears Roebuck catalog.

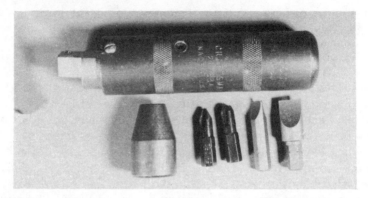

Fig. 2.4   The hand impact wrench for those stubborn fasteners.

Fig. 2.5   And for those super stubborn nuts, the nut cracker.

Fig. 2.6   Types of penetrating oil.

If neither of the preceding techniques appeals to you, try soaking the stubborn nut with a penetrating oil such as Mystery Oil or Liquid Wrench. Allow time for the oil to soak down into the threads. Using a box-end or socket wrench (an open-end wrench will only slip and ruin the nut and your knuckles), twist in *both* directions to tighten and loosen, keeping in mind that the first task is to break the seal. Do not use excessive force lest the shank of the bolt shear off and cause yet another problem. Use a propane gas torch to apply heat only to the nut so that it will expand more than the stud or bolt, then work the wrench back and forth to break the seal and allow the debris in the threads to loosen. If the nut still holds, get some modeling clay at a hobby shop and build a little dam around the offending nut and fill it with penetrating oil. Leave it overnight or for a day before trying again. If the nut has not broken loose, cut both sides of the nut off with a hacksaw and twist the remainder of the nut free with heavy vise-grip pliers or drift it off with a punch, hammer, or chisel.

Bolts

When the recalcitrant fastener is a bolt, the first method using the shock or impact wrench might work best. If the special tool needed is not available, some added measures are called for. Since the head of the bolt covers access to the threads for any penetrating oil, a small hole must be drilled at an angle, just deep enough to touch the threads. Form a modeling clay dam around the head of the bolt, adding enough oil to cover the drilled hole. The oil should be allowed to soak into the threads for a day or so. Set a socket or box-end wrench on the bolt head, hold the handle tightly and smartly rap the handle with a soft headed mallet in both the tightening and loosening directions to break the seal between the threads of the bolt and the threads of the hole.

When the nut is seized on a stud, the whole unit tends to back out of the engine before the nut will break loose. In this case, it is often best to discard the seized-up nut and stud and install new ones. If the stud itself is the problem, remove it with a tool designed for that purpose. The special tool does not mangle the stud and prevent its reuse. If you are willing to sacrifice the studs, they can be removed with the penetrating oil-heat technique and vise-grip pliers or small pipe wrench.

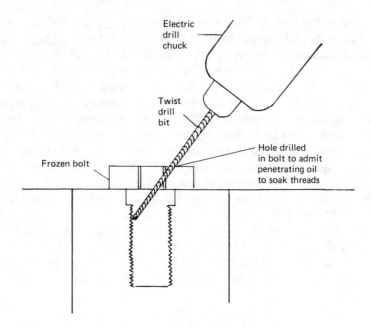

Fig. 2.7   Drilling a hole through the head of a frozen bolt may be the only way to get it loose.

Fig. 2.8   Stud removal tool.

Wood Screws

Much like the metal-to-metal fasteners, wood screws can also tighten up in the wood they are holding. This may be due to the use of a good marine glue in which they were originally set before being driven home or they may be rusted in. The first step is to carefully clean the screwdriver blade slot to provide a good grip for the removing tool. Break the seal by placing the blade of the heaviest screwdriver available in the slot and giving it a smart blow with a hammer. This will unseat the screw enough to back it out. Use the proper size screwdriver blade in a bit brace. Set the blade in the screw slot and rap the bit brace handle with the heel of your palm several times to start the screw backing out. Should the screw head shear off, drill out the remaining shank with a twist drill chucked in an electric or egg beater type hand drill. Try starting the drill hole with a very small drill, shifting to a shank-sized drill only after you have managed to get a hole started.

Machine Screws

For loosening machine screws, the heat and penetrating oil treatment is sometimes effective, but the hand-operated impact tool is still best. Breaking the seal of the threads with a sharp blow to a screwdriver set in the slot may be helpful. Care must be taken not to destroy the screwdriver slot by over-enthusiastic twisting. Brass, bronze, and aluminum screws are particularly susceptible to this problem.

Sheared Off Studs And Bolts

Sometimes, in spite of everything you have done to prevent it, a bolt or stud will shear off. Using a sharp pointed prick punch, set a drill point starter hole in the geometric center of the stud or bolt shank. Get a hole started with a small drill. Shift to a larger drill about half the size of the broken stud or bolt and drill

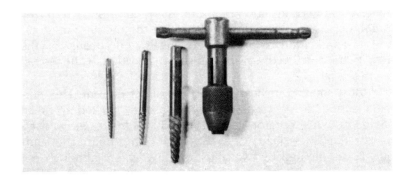

Fig. 2.9 Easy-out tool for the removal of sheared off bolts and studs.

the hole one-half inch deep (if possible), using lots of oil to help the drill bit. You'll have to buy, rent, or borrow a tool called "Easy-Out". When this tool is inserted into the drilled hole and rotated in a counterclockwise direction using a heavy wrench, the spiral teeth of the tool will engage the side of the hole in the stud or bolt and, aided with heat and more penetrating oil, will back out the offender.

Future Seize-Up Prevention

There are several preparations on the market that can be used to prevent (for the most part) this problem. However, none of these lasts too long, and they are expensive. You can try a good quality of graphite when you reattach any nuts, bolts, or screws, at least on the engine. Grease will ordinarily help unless the fastener is to be subjected to heat, in which case it will rapidly deteriorate. For threaded hose fittings you might try plumber's nylon thread tape which is good on fuel and water lines. The best aids to prevention (also the most difficult to install) are special "heli-coils" of rust- and corrosion-resistant metals which separate the threads of the stud or bolt from the element they are to fasten. One boat engine outdrive manufacturer has already begun to use these coils, but *only* on his outdrives.

THE ECLECTIC ELECTRIC TEST LAMP

If this gadget were running in a popularity contest among do-it-yourself skippers, it would be an easy winner. First and foremost, it is useful. It is also available everywhere. It is so simple in design and construction that it does not contribute to further maintenance problems. It is inexpensive to buy, easy to store, and its application to problem solving is limited only by the imagination of the user. The gadget in question is the home-made test lamp.

Most small craft have 12 volts of direct current (DC) normally supplied by a lead-acid storage battery backed up by an engine-driven alternator/generator. To make the tester, solder a pair of scrap wire leads to a 12-volt DC lamp bulb. The leads may be terminated by two alligator clips which, although not really needed, increase the usefulness of the tester. A socket can be used to hold the lamp but it is an unnecessary expense.

The test leads are best fabricated from rubber covered

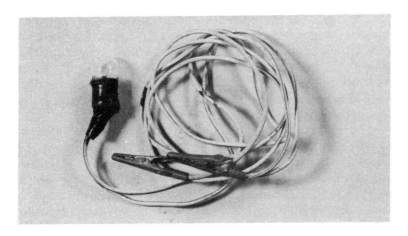

Fig. 2.10 The homemade 12-volt test lamp.

"Zip" cord or lamp cord. Make an initial cut to separate the two wires of the cord, then pull them apart to make two separate leads. The leads at the lamp end are stripped of insulation about an inch back and "tinned" with resin core solder and a soldering iron or small gas torch. Tinning makes the ends of the leads stiffer and permits them to be wrapped around the base of the lamp while the soldering is completed. The second lead is then soldered to the contact tip of the lamp. Plastic electrician's tape is used to insulate the base of the lamp and the soldered connections. The length of the test leads can suit your convenience. Solder two alligator type clips to the ends of the leads to complete the construction.

In the hands of an inspired improviser this device rates right along with the doctor's stethoscope in locating electrical problems. With the test lamp you can locate and diagnose such electrical problems as open circuits, shorted circuits, and high resistance circuits. You can use it to set time on the engine and test the performance of the alternator system. While it is not possible to take the exact measure of a voltage with it, you can get a fairly accurate reading by connecting the test lamp directly across the battery and observing the relative brilliance of the lamp when it lights. Next, connect it across the circuit under suspicion. If the lamp lights but with observably less brightness, it is safe to conclude there is some resistance that must be eliminated in the circuit.

When one of the small glass buss fuses prevalent on small craft blows, it is not easy to identify which one is blown except with the test lamp. When an open circuit is the problem, use the lamp to test several points back toward the battery until you find voltage present. From that point work back to the first point at which the voltage disappears. The open circuit must be between the two points.

Checking out proper operation of switches and solenoids is equally easy, and this is where the alligator clips are handy. To check a switch, connect one clip of the tester to any convenient negative or ground point. Next, touch the hot side of the switch with the other clip and observe whether the lamp lights. If it lights, the supply to the switch is OK—if not, you'll have to locate the point at which the supply is being lost. Next, with the switch in the OFF position touch the cold side of the switch with the lead. The lamp should *not* light. If you have a helper, have the switch moved to the ON position. If working alone, clip the test lead to the cold side of the switch. Hold the lamp where you can see it and move the switch to the ON position and the lamp will light if the switch is OK.

Solenoids (relays) usually make a distinct clicking sound when they are activated. This does not necessarily mean they are working properly. First, find out if voltage is getting to the operating coil of the relay by connecting one side of the test lamp to any convenient ground or negative point. On most relays there are two smaller connections (for the coil) and two larger connections that supply the heavier current. Connect the test lead of the lamp to each of the smaller connecting posts as the activating switch is operated. If sufficient voltage is being supplied to the relay coil, the lamp will light. Move the test lead to both sides of the heavier connection and again, if all is well, the lamp will light. If the lamp lights dimly, a high resistance contact has formed on the relay contact and it must either be replaced or disassembled and the contact cleaned. Unfortunately, most relays today are sealed and cannot be repaired. In Book 5, *Small Craft Electrical Maintenance*, we will give many more details on how to use the Eclectic Electric Test Lamp.

THE SPARKPLUG THREAD STARTER

On many inboard eight-cylinder and some six-cylinder engines the sparkplugs are hidden underneath the exhaust manifolds, as

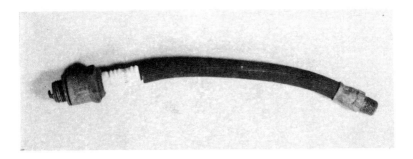

Fig. 2.11 The spark plug thread starter made from a length of old fuel hose.

they are on most automobiles. When you are changing spark-plugs or inspecting a faulty plug, it is often necessary to get the plugs started back into the threads of the sparkplug hole. It's difficult to do this by hand without cross-threading the plug, or burning yourself on the hot manifold. To avoid these problems, use a short piece of salvaged fuel line hose. Insert the wire-connecting end of the plug into the hose, which is used as an extender. Aided by a few drops of oil from the dip stick, the hose will grip the plug just enough to start it into the threads without letting it cross-thread.

ROLL-YOUR-OWN BUMP SWITCH

The bump switch is used by the professional mechanic to rotate the engine for short periods while the dwell is being checked, to set the distributor rotor for cam angle adjustment, and to test engine compression. It allows you to work at the engine without relying on an assistant (who cannot see what you are doing) to work the controls. These swiches can be purchased at most automotive supply stores. However, all that is needed to make your own is some sort of a momentary push-button switch that can carry several amps of current for short durations. Several types of switches will fill the bill including the push-button starter switches that can be purchased or salvaged, and the switches used to operate the tailgate window in station wagons, which are available at most automotive supply stores. Mount the switch in a plastic can that once held a 35MM film cartridge, using the cover as the mounting plate. Solder two heavy rubber-

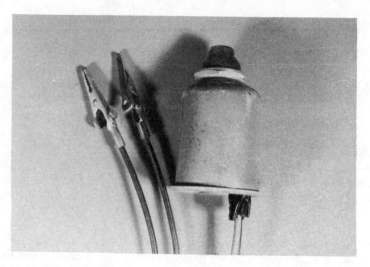

Fig. 2.12   This homemade inexpensive "bump" switch may not be pretty but it works.

covered flexible leads to the switch and two heavy clips to the ends of the leads. Tape the switch-holding plastic can with plastic electrician's tape.

The switch is simple to use. When you are preparing to set or check engine timing after replacing the point set and adjusting the dwell, you must first "bump" the engine a little at a time to line up the marks on the idler pulley and the calibrated marks usually found on the block. To time the engine these marks need to be cleaned and delineated with a piece of chalk or crayon. We have found it more convenient to paint these marks with a white stripe which shows clearly under the flashes of the timing light. Since you don't want the engine to start, leave the ignition switch in the OFF position and connect one lead of the bump switch to the nearest convenient positive voltage supply that connects directly to the battery; or connect the lead to the positive battery terminal. If your boat uses a starter assist relay, connect the other bump switch lead to one of the small solenoid connection posts. Make sure everything is clear to allow the engine to turn over and momentarily press the switch button. The starter assist relay should energize and the starter motor will turn. If it does not, change the switch lead to the second lead on the starter assist relay. Many boats do not have the starter assist relay and the connection of the bump switch is made to the starter relay, usually mounted on top of the starter motor. This relay also has two small posts, one connected to ground and the other connected by a long lead to the starter switch at the operating position. Connect the bump switch across the two posts and test for starter motor operation. If nothing happens, connect one lead of the switch to the battery (or the nearest positive supply) and the other to the relay coil connections. It is true that the commercial version of the bump switch, which is designed for heavy and continuous use, may be far more durable than the homemade version; but the homemade switch may be used only once a season and should last as long as you have use of it.

ROLL-YOUR-OWN GASKETS

In the course of disassembling, inspecting, and cleaning an element of the engine, a gasket may have to be replaced and the element reassembled. You should never try to reuse the old gaskets. In the replacement effort you have two options. You can identify the needed gasket by looking up the part number in the shop manual and buy it from the dealer, or you can make your own from gasket paper. Gasket paper is readily available from automotive supply stores and is easily cut to shape with a sharp pointed knife and scissors. The problem lies mostly in cutting it to the proper shape.

If during the disassembly you keep in mind that a new gasket is needed, extra care can be taken before the two parts that are to be gasketed are separated. Try to keep as much of the old gasket intact as possible because it can be used as a marking template for the new hand-cut gasket. When it is not possible to save the gasket, a marking template can be made from the part that will receive it. The smooth faced side of the metal part must be carefully cleaned of any remaining gasket material and sealing compound, then wire-brushed and polished with crocus cloth. Lightly coat the face of the part with grease and press down on the gasket paper sheet. Remove the part carefully so as not to smear the greasy outline of the gasket. Next, cut away all the ungreased paper using a mat knife or scissors. Remember to use gasket sealing compound before joining the two parts connected by the gasket.

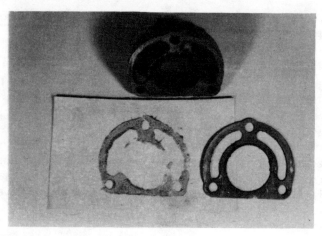

Fig. 2.13   Making a gasket from a grease outline.

LUBE OIL DRAINING TRICKS

This is one of the easiest (and often messiest) ways that the PPM skipper can save maintenance costs on his boat. If the job is turned over to a professional, he will have to charge the same hourly labor rate as if he were doing a highly technical carburetor or ignition fix. You can do the job yourself at substantial savings with the knowledge that the job has been done correctly. Listed are several steps that the professional might skip because he could not afford to charge for them.

The first money-saving step is to buy your lubrication oil in case lots—watch the papers for sales at large automotive supply stores (usually at the end of the season). You can save 50 percent or better over the individual can price at the local marina or gas dock. In most instances, the oil on sale is a nationally-known brand and is therefore reliable. Buy the oil recommended by the engine maker (check your owner's manual). Generally, a lighter weight oil is recommended for the colder northern waters, and a correspondingly heavier oil for the southern and warmer waters.

When you buy your oil, see if the oil filter your engine uses is also on sale. Look up the type oil filter in your owner's manual and cross index it at the store with several other brands of filters. There is often a wide price variation between filter brands, all (or most) of which do the same job in the same way. In addition to the filter element, pick up an inexpensive filter removal

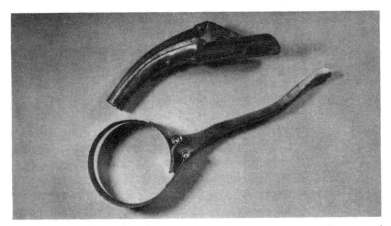

Fig. 2.14   Pictured here, a low cost oil filter strap-wrench and oil can punch spout.

Fig. 2.15   An electric drill-driven oil pump for draining oil through dip stick hole.

wrench and an oil can punch spout. These tools, although of nonprofessional quality, will last indefinitely for the individual user (and to make this investment really pay off, change the oil and filter on your car as well as your boat).

Draining of old oil out of your inboard engine is complicated by the location of the engine oil drain plug which, of necessity, is located at the lowest point of the engine on the oil sump pan. The inaccessible location makes it difficult to get a wrench on it or to put a catch pan under it to drain the old oil into. This may be the primary reason that this task is avoided by many skippers. Lately marine engine makers have installed a hose fitting on the dip stick tube so that a drain suction pump can be easily attached to pump the oil out. The problem may be in finding the pump with the proper hose fittings. However, in many hardware and marine supply stores, you can purchase an inexpensive small plastic pump which is driven by an electric drill. The price of the pump will negate the initial savings of doing the job yourself, but subsequent uses will amortize its cost.

If you decide against the pump, you will still need something to fit under the engine to catch the old oil. Here the problem is to find something that will fit under the engine that also can be removed without spilling the dirty oil into the bilge. Of course you can consider bailing the old oil out of the catch pan into a second container, but the easiest method is to use two heavy-grade plastic trash bags, one inside the other. The bags are easily fitted under the engine and positioned open under the drain plug. An assistant holds one side of the bags open while you hold the other and remove the drain plug with a wrench. (Remember that you are looking down on the engine and that the drain plug works in the opposite direction to which it would if you were underneath the engine looking up.) It is best to loosen the plug just enough with the wrench to be able to turn the balance by hand without dropping it into the bilge. Allow the old oil to drain completely into the plastic bags and replace the drain plug finger-tight to avoid cross-threading the plug. Before securing the plug, pass your side of the bags of drained oil to your helper, who can maneuver them out from under the engine so that they do not tear. The bags will lift out of the bilges through the smallest of holes and should not cause any messy oil spills in the bilge.

Whatever method you select to drain the oil, first start and run the engine to bring the oil up to operating temperature, thus allowing the oil to drain more easily. This procedure is an *absolute* requirement if you are going to pump the oil out. If the boat is out of the water, provide water by hose to cool the engine while you are warming up the oil.

After the oil has been drained from the crankcase and oil sump, the next step is to remove the old oil filter. With the possible exception of some six-cylinder in-line engines, the oil filter element is, like the drain plug, rarely located conveniently and is difficult to remove and replace. In the removal process there is the likelihood of another mess due to the old oil remaining in the filter after the engine has been shut down. In addition, the remaining oil in the filter may be under a slight pressure due to the action of the oil pressure regulating valve. To prevent a pint or so of dirty oil from gushing out when the filter is first loosened with the filter strap wrench, punch a hole in the *bottom* of the thin-walled filter with a screw driver and let the remaining oil drain into a pan or plastic bag before removing the filter. Or, while holding a bag or container underneath, remove the filter and let the excess oil drain. In any case, have a lot of rags or paper towels ready and wipe up *all* oil spills immediately. The filter strap wrench will loosen the filter enough so that it can be turned out by hand. As soon as the old filter has been removed, replace it with a new one. Don't forget to rub the rubber gasket on the top of the new filter with a finger full of oil so that it will seat properly and not leak. Screw in the new filter cartridge tightly by hand. It is rarely necessary to tighten it with the filter wrench.

With the oil drained and a new filter installed the next step is to install the new oil. From the owner's manual you can determine the number of quarts (or liters) of oil needed to fill the engine and the oil filter. Using your new punch spout, replace the old oil. Start and warm the engine. As the engine is idling, check for leaks around the new oil filter, tightening it as needed. Shut down the engine and check the engine oil level with the dip stick to make sure the oil is at the proper level.

The entire operation can be simplified if you purchase and install a special oil drain hose and stop valve at the bottom of the engine. This device is commercially available but somewhat expensive. You can roll your own if you are willing to take the time. A good quality bronze plug is needed to replace the drain plug. The bronze plug is tapped for a hose fitting and a length of neoprene hose (such as might be used with fuel lines). A valve fitting is installed on the other end of the hose. The type of fitting is determined by whether you choose to pump the old oil out or simply lead the hose out through the bilge drain plug and let the oil drain out of the engine through the drain hose into a container. When not in use the oil drain hose is valved shut and held in position with a clamp on the inside of the transom. This arrangement is neat and convenient once it has been installed.

TESTING THERMOSTATS AND
OVERTEMP SENSING SWITCHES

The thermostat in a marine engine has two functions—first, it aids in bringing the engine up to operating temperature quickly, and second, it regulates the operating temperature of the engine by sensing the temperature of the coolant and opening and closing automatically to divert the coolant as required to maintain engine temperature under varying loads. Normally the thermostat is a very reliable and simple device, operating under an expanding bellows principle. In the marine environment, however, it may not always function as it should. This is particularly true when the cooling liquid is raw sea water which acts on the metal device.

Most skippers will simply remove and replace the stat with a new one rather than take time to test it. However, it may not be the fault of the stat at all but something else in the cooling system. To save the needless effort and expense of replacing it, it is easy to test the stat and determine if it is doing the job. First, remove and set aside the thermostat housing retaining bolts. Tap the housing lightly with a block of wood or the handle of a screwdriver to break it loose from its gasket. It is not necessary to remove the connecting hoses from the housing. (Never try to use an old gasket again. Unless you intend to buy a new gasket, carefully remove the old one so that it can be used as a template for cutting a new gasket.) Lift the thermostat out of the housing and carefully inspect the inner area of the thermostat housing. Look for accumulated dirt and debris that might have forced the stat up out of its seat. Clean, scrape, and burnish the mating faces of the housing. In the owner's manual, look up the operating temperature of your engine. Many stats are designed to open at 160°F, but some of the newer engines are designed to open at somewhat higher temperatures.

Once out of the engine, the stat *must be closed*. If it is jammed in the open position replace it immediately. Place the stat in a pan of just enough water to completely cover it. Put a cooking thermometer in the pan of water and heat. Observe the action of the stat as the thermometer approaches the operating temperature. It should open fully. Next, add cold water to the pan and again watch to see that the stat closes. If the stat opens and closes as it should with the temperatures registered, it may be replaced in the housing. Install a new gasket with gasket ce-

Fig. 2.16   Thermostat test set up. Can also be done on the stove.

ment. Seat the stat in the housing, install the housing cover, and torque up the retainer bolts. Start and run the engine up to operating temperature and check for coolant leaks around the housing, retightening the retainer bolts as needed.

It is relatively easy to test the engine coolant temperature sender, if it is the switch type which lights a warning lamp at the operating position. It is more difficult to test the type that causes a meter to read the actual temperature at the operating position. To test the switch type, disconnect the electrical lead, which is usually mounted close to the thermostat. Back the switch body out of its housing with a wrench. With a CEE clamp attach the switch to the side of a small saucepan with the electric connector up out of the water. Fill the pan with enough water to cover the sensing section of the switch and put a cooking thermometer into the pan with the switch. Connect an ohmmeter to the electrical connection on the switch and attach the other meter lead to the body of the switch or pan with a clip. If you do not have an ohmmeter, use a test lamp and a battery to get a positive indication when the switch closes and opens. Heat the water and observe the temperature on the thermometer at the point that the ohmmeter reads "continuity" (complete circuit) or the lamp lights. These temperatures are specified in the engine shop manual or ask your dealer for the information.

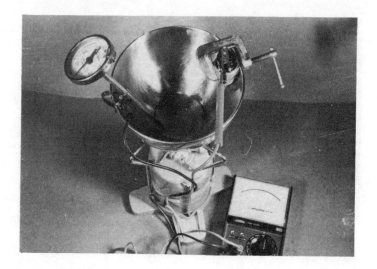

Fig. 2.17   A test set-up showing coolant overtemperature sensing switch.

(A typical value is 190°F.) The meter or lamp should not indicate at this point as the switch should be open. The value may
be plus or minus another five degrees as these switches are not
precision devices. At 200° or up to 205°, the ohmmeter should
read or the test lamp should light indicating that the sender is
OK. When the sender is the variable resistance type, driving a
direct reading temperature gauge on the operating position, the
test set-up is the same but *only* the ohmmeter will indicate
proper operation. Set the ohmmeter to the thousand ohms scale
and bring the water in the pan up to 220°. At this temperature
the ohmmeter should read 448 ohms plus or minus 5 percent.
The small meter is an invaluable tool for the PPM skipper, and it
is versatile and inexpensive.

These tests can be accomplished in yet another way which
does not involve the removal and replacement of any of the devices unless proven faulty. The testing devices are "melt sticks"
which are composed of a material that melts at specific temperatures when pressed against the metal of the thermostat housing. You might be able to find these sticks at an automotive supply store that specializes in tools as well as parts.

Fig. 2.18 This small inexpensive pocket volt-ohmmeter has many uses on a small craft.

SMALL CRAFT BATTERY PREVENTIVE MAINTENANCE

We have described the lead-acid battery in a small craft as one of the major soft spots. This analysis is supported by Coast Guard statistics, which indicate that by far the greatest number of calls for assistance are due to dead batteries.

For the small craft skipper, batteries, like most of the equipment below decks, are out of sight, out of mind. Yet, in the operation of a small craft (other than sail-powered) what, if anything, is more crucial? Even after the engine has started, the battery is still necessary to complete the electrical current circuit even though the generator/alternator is carrying a major portion of the electrical load.

To apply preventive maintenance procedures to the battery, first gather a few tools. You will need a box-end wrench of the proper size to loosen the battery cable clamps; fresh water and a strong detergent soap; a small amount of baking soda; a hydrometer (inexpensive and invaluable); a supply of *distilled* water; nonmetallic sandpaper or wire brush; and a little Vaseline or light grease.

Uncover the battery, and loosen and remove the *negative* (−) terminal cable clamp *first* to prevent any severe flaming arcs and possible damage to the battery if the wrench slips. If it is not already marked, cut a negative sign (−) in the terminal of the battery *and* in the cable clamp at this time. Use a screwdriver and tap a negative sign in the soft metal of the clamp and post. Cut a positive sign (+) in the positive terminal and cable clamp. It will help to assure that the cables are always connected correctly. Next, remove the battery and give it a thorough bath. The battery functions in a hostile environment—salt air leaves a harmful coating on the battery and because of its proximity to the engine it also gets a coating of greasy (and often electrically conductive) dirt. In addition, when the battery is on charge, the vents emit vapors of hydrogen, oxygen, and sulphuric gases as a natural result of the electrolysis that goes on inside the battery. These gases tend to combine with air to form unwelcome chemicals that leave deposits on the outside of the battery, particularly on the terminals. All of these deposits can form electric current leakage paths on the surface of the battery and will cause the stored charge to run down when the battery is not in use. Other deposits will form high-resistance coatings between the terminals and the cable clamps and prevent enough current from reaching the starter motor, which demands huge amounts of amperes.

Scrub the battery thoroughly with soap and water and a stiff brush, being careful not to get any soap or water in the vent holes in the caps. Rinse the battery off with clear fresh water, then give it a second rinse with a tablespoon of baking soda dissolved in a cup of water. This will neutralize any acid remaining on the top and sides of the battery. Remove the filler caps (if you have them) one by one and make sure the vents are clear by poking through them with a small piece of copper wire. Check the specific gravity reading of each cell, adding in the temperature compensation as directed by the instructions with the hydrometer, and enter the results in the engine log. This will aid in predicting when the battery must be replaced. Any significant variations in the reading indicate that a cell may be going sour. If *one* cell goes, the whole battery goes. We keep a small floating ball type of hydrometer stored right on top of the battery at all times. While not as accurate as the numerical reading hydrometers, it helps us to keep a proper eye on the condition of the battery.

Fig. 2.19   Baby (battery) gets a thorough bath in soap and water.

Fig. 2.20   Then a baking soda rinse for that final touch.

Fig. 2.21   Check the gas vents to make sure they are not plugged.

Fig. 2.22   Checking the specific gravity with a hydrometer.

Fig. 2.23   Top off each cell with DISTILLED water.

Top off each cell with distilled water so that the electrolyte (the liquid in the battery) just covers the tops of the plates—nothing ruins a battery more quickly than dry plates. You can find distilled water in most drug stores. Do not use local tap water, which may contain iron, metallic salts, and silt and may shorten the battery's life. When a battery fails, it is generally because a coating of sulphates and other material on the plates has increased the internal impedance (resistance to current flow) of the battery. Don't overfill the battery—the electrolyte

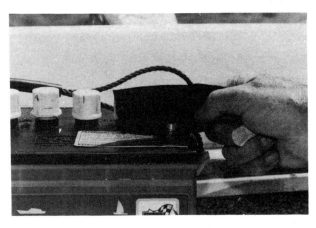

Fig. 2.24   Clean and burnish the terminals.

expands during the charge due to gas bubbles and will spill out of the vents to cause considerable trouble.

Before reinstalling the battery, check the battery hold-downs for rust and corrosion. Wire-brush and lightly grease if required. If you keep your battery in a battery box, give the box a good wash and rinse also.

Wire-brush and burnish with sandpaper both the battery terminals and the cable clamps, paying particular attention to the *inside* contacting surface of the cable clamps. If there are any white, crystal-like deposits on the cable clamps, rinse the clamps in water with baking soda after the polishing. If available, install anti-corrosion felt pads on the battery terminals. Soak these pads in a chemical that will help prevent resistance-forming deposits on the terminals.

Reconnect the cables, beginning with the positive (+) cable. Tighten the clamp bolts and give the terminal a light coating of Vaseline or grease to protect it from oxygen. To do a complete job, do not reconnect the battery until you have removed, burnished, and reconnected the opposite ends of the cables to the starter and engine block. If the preceding procedures seem too elaborate, keep in mind that they need to be done only once or, at most, twice a season. In between times, simple inspections will suffice.

In the off season, store the battery out of the boat on a wooden block away from any cement. Give the battery a final charge and, if you have one, keep it on a trickle charger from time to time. A charged battery will tolerate extremely low temperatures and can be used during the winter as a booster starting battery for your car.

EXHAUST MANIFOLD PREVENTIVE MAINTENANCE

Exhaust manifolds, like the battery, are subjected to extremes in the operating environment. They are expensive to replace and, because they are often made of cast iron, cannot easily be repaired. The determined PPM skipper can do much to preserve and protect the manifolds. Unfortunately, the following procedures involve a lot of drudgery, as do so many small craft preventive maintenance tasks. Keep in mind that these investments of your time will always pay off in better performance and long-term cost savings.

The majority of manifolds are fabricated of cast iron and are attached to the engine block with threaded studs and hex nuts, and lock washers or flat washers. Due to the extremes of both heat and the cooling water (especially salt water) these fasteners tend to seize up. The manifolds themselves often come assembled in sections, joined together with more nuts and bolts with gaskets at the joining sections. The protective paint, also subjected to the operating extremes, rapidly deteriorates and ceases to protect. As a result, the paint also must be restored with substantial and careful preparation.

Following are the steps for the removal, rodding out, cleaning, derusting, regasketing, reassembly, and installation of a typical set of exhaust manifolds for a V-8 marine inboard engine. The best time to carry out this task is at the end of the season when the boat has been brought ashore and buttoned up for the winter.

The manifolds can be removed after the engine oil and filter have been changed and the engine has been flushed with fresh water and completely drained at the block drains. The manifolds can be brought home and worked on during the off season. Be sure to give the exhaust ports and all fittings a light coating of rust-preventing oil, and stuff oil-soaked rags into the ports to keep out damp air.

Removing the manifolds may require the following tools: a combination box-end wrench and open-end wrench for the mounting bolts, a can of penetrating oil, a gas torch, and modeling clay (the last three items are needed if one or more nuts or bolts has seized up). You also will need the following materials: a full set of gaskets or gasket paper and gasket-sealing compound, wire brushes (both hand- and power-driven), sanding discs for a powered disc sander of the type used in an autobody shop, and a can of caustic soda such as Draino. The caustic is optional and there will be other methods suggested. If the manifolds are very rusty, you will require naval jelly and chemical paint removers. You will also need a small supply of metal priming paint, such as a good quality heat-resistant wash primer, and one or more spray cans of engine paint.

Begin the manifold removal process by detaching the coolant hoses. Inspect the hose ends and plan to replace those that are worn. If you have any of the ring type hose clamps, remove and discard them and replace with screw type stainless steel clamps. Give each of the mounting bolts or nuts a liberal dose of penetrating oil and let them soak in it for several minutes. Remove the nuts and bolts using the box-end wrench, since it is less likely to slip and mangle your knuckles and the face of the nut or bolt. For seized-up nuts and bolts, refer to the earlier section in this chapter. Set the nuts and bolts aside in a small container of oil. Replace any that are badly rusted or corroded. Drain any remaining water from the manifolds and take them home. Remember, manifolds fabricated of cast iron are often as brittle as glass and must be handled with care.

Once the manifolds ar home you can disassemble them at leisure. Use a sharp thin-bladed knife to peel the old gaskets from the intersecting faces of the manifold assembly, unless you have already purchased a set of precut gaskets. If you are going to cut your own gaskets, save the old ones for marking templates. Once the manifolds are disassembled, the next task is to rod out the inside *water* passages with a brass welding rod or a flat soft steel bar which has been slightly bent at one end so that it will act as a scraper when you push it through the passages. There are two alternatives to cleaning out the water passages. You can dam up one end of a water passage with a whittled block of wood and fill the passage with a mixture of caustic soda and water, allowing it to soak overnight; or you can take them to an automotive radiator repair shop to be boiled out in one of their cleaning tanks. As a rule, the fee is modest, since the manifold sections can be left unattended in the tank overnight, but be sure to inquire as to the charge first. This soaking and boiling out does not eliminate the rodding-out

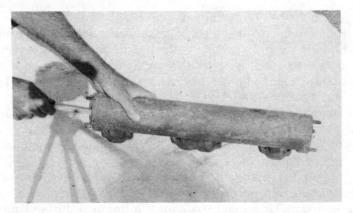

Fig. 2.25   In rodding out a manifold, either a flat steel rod or welding rod can be used.

requirement but loosens the debris and allows you to get more unwanted material out of the water passages.

Once the insides of the manifolds are as clean as possible it is time to start on the outside. If the manifolds were boiled out at the radiator shop, most of the remaining paint will have loosened, and you will only have to wirebrush and burnish them down to shiny bare metal. If you plan to do the whole job yourself use naval jelly on the rust and chemical paint remover on the remaining paint. An alternative is to have the manifold sections cleaned at a shop that provides sand blasting services. Ask the shop to give the water passages a few blasts of sand also. By whatever method suits you, get the outside of the manifolds clean to bare metal. From this point on, do not handle the manifold sections with your bare hands because the oil from your hands will prevent priming paint from sticking. Before you start to paint the manifolds carefully wash them with a degreasing agent such as acetone. Use a good quality zinc chromate wash primer and give the metal two coats according to the instructions on the container.

Using old wire coat hangers for suspension hooks, hang the manifold sections up in the open air and spray paint them with heat-resistant engine paint that is available in almost any automotive or hardware store. Give each section as many coats as there is paint in the cans. This is an easy and quick method of painting and this type of paint normally dries very quickly so that you can put on several coats in a day.

Fig. 2.26 Manifolds cleaned, burnished and ready for priming coats.

Fig. 2.27 The refurbished manifolds with extended lifespan.

When the paint has set and dried completely you can begin reassembling the manifold sections. If you are cutting and forming your own gaskets, follow the suggestions in this chapter. In any case, be sure to add gasket sealer to the gaskets and set them on the section interfaces. Install and moderately tighten the nuts and bolts. (When the manifolds are back on the engine and in use, you will have to retighten them to prevent leaks as they expand under heat.) Wrap the manifolds in old rags and store them. This task may be required only once or twice during the life of the engine but will significantly extend the life of the very expensive manifolds.

3
PLANNING A PREVENTIVE MAINTENANCE PROGRAM FOR SMALL CRAFT ENGINES

PLANNING AIDS

Planning a preventive maintenance program of *any* kind requires, first and foremost, facts—*hard* data acquired by inspection, testing, and most important, record-keeping. No commercial or military vessel goes to sea without a daily or hourly log that records even the most mundane and routine events. From these logs, shipboard managers can formulate preventive maintenance activities and plans.

Devices

In addition to paper forms, there are various devices to aid in the collection of hard data. One of the most valuable of these is the engine hour meter, similar to an automotive use time meter (odometer), which registers the number of miles that the car has traveled and is a fair representation of the time the engine (and the whole car) has been in use. Although there are instruments that record the distance traveled by a boat, few small craft carry them. Not only are they very expensive, but they are primarily for navigation purposes—not maintenance record-keeping. The engine hour meter is of greater use and much less expensive. This device is no more than an electrical clock that is connected to the *cold* (or de-energized) side of the ignition switch and records the time that the ignition switch is in the ON position. The read-out is in the form of digits that indicate the hours and minutes that the engine has been in operation.

The importance of recording engine use time in small craft (as far as a preventive maintenance plan goes) cannot be over-emphasized. Unlike an automobile engine, a boat engine

Fig. 3.1   Examples of elapsed time indicators for monitoring engine use time.

in gear, with the propeller spinning, is under stress at *all* times. When the propeller is turning, the marine engine is operating on the stress level of an automobile engine in second gear climbing a steep hill. This is the principal reason that automotive engines converted to marine use are often less than satisfactory. Outboard engines are designed with this stress in mind. The reason for the increasing popularity of the marine diesel engine is that it's rugged to begin with. This is why we emphasize the necessity for keeping a good record of engine use time for your boat. To this end, there are available several types of engine hour meters (12 volts DC) that cost around $25, are easy to install, and will provide the invaluable information you need.

A less expensive method of recording engine use time involves salvaging an automotive electric clock from the junk yard. Take pains to protect the workings of the clock from the normal damp and salty atmosphere of the boat. The clock need not be mounted on the dash or in operating position since the information that is displayed need only be recorded from time to time. The principal limitation of these clocks is that they record only twelve hours at a time. As soon as eleven hours and a few minutes of running time have been recorded, you will have to make an entry in the engine log.

There are also electro-chemical devices that are simple, reasonably accurate, relatively inexpensive, and very easy to install. These gadgets, like the clocks, are connected to the cold side of the ignition switch. In one type, current flow through an electrolyte causes a coating to form on a calibrated glass column. At the end of the time period the device is removed from its clips, reversed, and the process starts over again. In another type current causes a color change to take place after a certain period of time. One of the simpler versions of the second type is shown. In the example, the "elapsed time indicator" changes color after fifty hours of current flow. The time period after which the color changes can be adjusted by adding various values of series resistance with the device to control the magnitude of current flow. The tiny bulb must be renewed each time the color changes.

The Log Book

A log is the least expensive and the most troublesome method of recording engine use time. The entries must be faithfully and accurately kept. An entry must be made *each* time the engine is started and put in gear and each time the engine is secured. The engine use time log book also serves as a record book for all sorts of maintenance data. For example, all small craft should have a tachometer and a table calibrated for speed through the water and over the ground versus engine RPM for a given load and water currents. To accomplish this, all that is needed is a stop watch and a tachometer. The boat is run on a range between two static objects (usually ashore) known to be *exactly*

Fig. 3.2   An engine use time log.

one mile apart. (Many small craft charts will show ranges ashore that are to be used primarily for this purpose.) With such a table calibrated and entered in the engine-use log, you can determine your *Speed over Ground* (SOG) with very good accuracy—good enough for inshore piloting anyway.

In order to carry out a maintenance task you will often need some small bit of essential data—such as the degrees of dwell required for the point set of the spacing, the plug gap size, the type and model of the oil filter required, the torque in foot pounds for the head bolts, and all manner of adjustment and control specifications. All of these can be entered in a table in the log book so that you need only go to the log book for any information needed. You can also record names, addresses, and telephone numbers of sources of supplies and parts in the log. List technicians' and mechanics' names and addresses. Dates of purchase and amounts of fuel bought for tax rebate purposes should be entered since the tax on gasoline in many states is rebatable to boat owners because they do not use the highways for which the tax was imposed in the first place.

Even though an engine use time device is available, the engine log is still required if any hard-headed maintenance planning is to be done. Small hardcover notebooks can be picked up in any stationery store, and the type that suits you best is the one that will work most satisfactorily as long as you are faithful about keeping it up to date.

Inspection Checklists

If we have persuaded you at least to try an engine log for one season, there is one thing more for you to do. Make up a set of inspection sheets that, for convenience, can also be put in the back of the log. These checklists and the data collected and entered on them will form the basis of your personal PPM program. Making up checklists is easy. Start with the lubrication checklist using the engine owner's manual. Next, using the engine subsystems chart in Chapter 1, list the maintenance "soft spots." As you go through these systems, try to think of anything that *might* go wrong. Often a one word cue is enough to remind you to check that point on the engine. The checklists need not be elaborate—just thorough. Best of all, once they have been made up they can be used over and over. In addition, a good list can be modified to include or exclude data as your use of the checklist indicates.

PLAN DESIGNING FOR PPM

It is all very well to mentally formulate plans, but they must be committed to paper in an orderly form so that they can be revised and reordered to better suit changing conditions. In the preceding section, we described various devices and methods of collecting engine use time data to be used *primarily* for the more routine kinds of preventive maintenance. Any other preventive maintenance can only be determined by periodic and thorough inspection programs.

The inspection program plan must be formulated. The main consideration is *when* to inspect. The question may be answered by the owner's manual, which includes a periodic lubrication program (usually in the form of a list, chart, or diagram). The program has been developed by engineers who have carefully studied data on engine subsystem failures and other in-use performance data. Based upon this data, they develop a lubrication periodic program, which, if followed by the owner, will assure the greatest reliability of performance by the engine. However there is no way the factory engineers can guarantee against failure attributed to the extreme stress, metal fatigue, heat, and vibration that is placed on a marine engine. Only a good PPM inspection program will help in this case.

Incipient mechanical failure is very often signaled *before* it happens. Many things on the engine will send out loud and distinct distress calls well before they give up the ghost. For example, an engine that starts with difficulty and misfires or idles poorly after it starts may be signaling that one or more of its sparkplugs have gone sour and warning you to locate the faulty plugs and replace them *immediately*. A loose water pump/alternator drive belt squeals. Two metal surfaces in need of lubrication make hideous grating noises. Loose and vibrating connections on hoses, junctions, and fuel lines corrode and leak to indicate their poor connection. Professional mechanics often use an equivalent of a doctor's stethoscope to locate and identify a malfunctioning part that emits faint but important noises. You can check a suspected problem point by placing the blade of a long screwdriver on the point under suspicion and putting your ear directly against the end of the handle. Noises, often masked by other engine sounds, are transmitted up the handle directly to your ear.

The lubrication plan in the owner's manual can be used, in part, to develop your PPM inspection program. As you carry out the lubrication of various points on the engine (inboard or outboard) carefully check all the points in the system you are lubricating for signs of potential malfunction.

The Inspection Checklist

A more thorough inspection program can be easily developed into an inspection checklist by considering each of the engine's subsystems as described in Chapter 1 and listing all the things that *might* go wrong in those subsystems. Then note a checkpoint within the system that can be inspected or tested to give you *hard* data indicating whether or not that point needs immediate attention.

Although checklists may be tedious, all pilots cheerfully carry them out for they are up in that airplane with the passengers. The small craft skipper is out on the boat along with any passengers and also owes homself the reassurance that comes from knowing that the boat's engine is reliably ready for sea.

We do not propose that the entire propulsion system be totally inspected before each use of the boat. That, you should pardon the expression, would be going overboard. Regular and periodic inspection based upon in-use time is the easiest and most practical method—and effective if faithfully followed.

The following is a *model* of a pre-season checklist for that major trouble spot—the engine ignition system. Let me emphasize that this applies to the *pre-season* and is only a model. Such a detailed inspection and test should not be necessary *during* the season when quick but careful examination of the ignition system components will suffice.

Pre-season Engine ignition system checklist

1. Remove and inspect the condition of each spark.
   (Note: Sparkplugs can be "read" and often indicate, by their condition, a malfunction *elsewhere* in the engine.)
2. Check plug electrode gap and adjust as required, clean and file electrodes.
3. Inspect ignition high voltage harness.
   (Note: Look for cracked or worn insulation, proper "dressing" of the leads away from hot spots

and grounds. Pay close attention to the insulation of the plug wire holders.)

4. Inspect and clean ignition coil, high voltage tower and low voltage connections. Look for signs of looseness and corrosion.

5. Inspect and clean outside of distributor cap. Look for signs of cracks, dirt and corrosion within the individual towers holding the plug wires.

6. Remove and inspect the inside of the distributor cap. Look for signs of moisture, cracks in the insulation, signs of wear and carbon on the electrical contacts.

7. Remove and inspect the distributor rotor. Look for dirt and corrosion, cracks in the insulation, clean and burnish all metal connections. Consider total replacement.

8. Inspect the condition of the contact faces of the point set. Look for evidence of burns, pits, and excessive wear. Consider replacement.

9. Inspect the condition of the point set rubbing block, and the lubrication pad. Look for excessive wear and lack of lubrication.

10. Inspect all low voltage connections within the distributor.

11. Inspect the condition of the automatic advance weights and springs. Look for rust, proper lubrication and freedom of action.

12. *Test* point gap with flat feeler gauge.
    (Note: "Bump" engine over until points are wide open. Set or check gap from engine specifications. Proper gap sets both dwell and time on engine.)

13. Lubricate all points on distributor as required by owner's manual.

14. *Test* timing of engine with timing light.

This model could be used by any skipper making his own checklist. Some of the checkpoints require more than a cursory glance. Some of the checks and inspections will require the use of tools and test instruments as well as some materials. The same list can be used (with modifications) during the season for periodic spot inspections and should, for the most part, eliminate the more elaborate testing and be limited to the visual inspection.

Once you have made up a set of checklists for *each* of the subsystems of the engine, do not consider them as inviolate—modify, add and delete checks and inspections as experience dictates. Try to keep the lists from being too wordy. Often a one-word cue will be enough.

Data-Gathering And Analysis

With the inspection checklists roughed in, ask someone to help you by reading off the checkpoints as you carry out the actual inspection, and noting what you find during the inspection. When the inspection has been completed and all of the data has been gathered, assimilate the information before you begin to formulate your preventive maintenance *plan*.

Essentially, the PPM program is little more than taking the hard data collected during the inspection and answering questions such as: What has to be done? When should it be done? In what order should it be done? What tools and materials (parts) are required? Where can they be obtained at the best price? Should they be purchased or made?

By answering all of these questions and making notes on the information accumulated you will find that most of all preventive maintenance tasks will go smoothly and can be carried out with a minimum of time, effort, and expense. This is where the PPM program pays off. Before you carry out a specific maintenance task, try our system of job analysis. Use the owner's manual with this text and determine what steps will be required to complete the task. By viewing the tasks as a series of steps and listing tools and materials, you avoid most of the time-wasting inefficiencies.

Shopping For Materials And Services

Comparison shop for materials and services and look for sales as suggested in Chapter 1. Careful shopping can be applied to many needs, such as ignition parts. There is yet little difference between inboard engine ignition systems and automotive ignitions. Some, but not all, outboards (especially the larger engines) use conventional automotive ignition systems and parts.

However, when the parts or the materials required are those that are specifically designed or formulated for marine application, shoreside substitutes *rarely* will do the job—so don't practice foolish economy. Shop around but stick to the best quality marine supplies.

You might consider starting a collection of marine supplies catalogs. Some, not all, catalogs give very good price breaks on simple hardware. Good quality marine hardware at a reasonable price is not always easy to find. Almost any boating or yachting magazine will have ads for free or nominally priced catalogs.

If your engine is a nationally distributed brand, do not expect to be able to find any bargains in parts and supplies because the manufacturers protect their dealers by restricting the distribution of these parts. While your engine is under warranty we recommend that you use only those parts distributed by the engine maker through authorized dealers. When the warranty runs out, you can shop around for a better deal. Whenever you are having a problem with your engine or difficulty obtaining a part, write to the Customer Service Representative of the company that manufactured the engine. As a rule, he can assist you in solving the problem.

Still another excellent source of information on parts, materials, and services is the yellow pages of the telephone directory. However, consider this word of advice before you talk to anyone on the telephone. Have at hand a complete description of the part, the model and year of the engine and the part number (from your owner's or shop manual). Any information that descibes the needed item will save time on the phone and help often busy counter clerks to locate and identify it.

A number of free-lance mechanics have appeared on the boating scene—probably due to the high costs of parts and labor. As a rule they do not advertise except by word of mouth. Use great caution before employing these free-lancers to work on your engine. Check their credentials by asking other skippers if they were satisfied with their work.

Drafting Your Personal PPM Program

To design the plan that best suits you and your boat, follow these six discreet steps:

Step 1   Gather all the facts concerning *what* maintenance is needed. To keep this as effortless as possible, use the inspection checklists you have made.

Step 2   List the maintenance tasks needed, drawing information from the inspection checklists and notes on observations made during the inspections. Using the list of tasks, assign priority to each task, then reorder the tasks.

Step 3   Try doing a job analysis on any task that appears to involve a number of steps. Think the job through first and jot down the steps in an ordered sequence. Often the analysis will show that a step is out of sequence, and it is far better to have discovered it on paper than later when the actual task is underway. Allocate time requirements to each task and assume conditions. As a rule, engine maintenance tasks are not subject to weather restrictions. However, it is best to be prepared for some personal discomfort caused by foul weather.

Step 4   List any tools, parts, and materials needed and note potential sources to procure them. Keep in mind that a significant portion of the time allocated to a maintenance task can be consumed by unplanned running around to find supplies.

Step 5   Schedule the tasks. This is not as easy as it might seem, for there will be many things competing for your time. If you have done a good job on your task-time allocation you will not make the mistake of scheduling a task that takes several hours to be done in less than a half day.

Step 6   Carry out the actual maintenance tasks following the plan.
      You must not consider any of the foregoing as rigid doctrine. Adopt and modify all or part to suit your temperament, skills, and resources. The object is to make the plan a personal one—one that is yours and yours alone. By following your *own* plan, rather than someone else's, there's a better chance that you'll actually achieve your objectives.

4
SMALL CRAFT ENGINE SPARES AND MATERIALS FOR A PPM PROGRAM

In this chapter we will suggest a number of spares and materials which long experience has proven are most often needed to maintain a small craft propulsion system, be it a two-cycle outboard or a four-cycle inboard engine. We list general suggestions for the small craft skipper who boats on a lake or river, or who makes overnight or week-end salt water trips along shore. Your boating environment will dictate for the most part what spares and materials *you should* carry. Skippers who operate boats on lakes and rivers perhaps require no on-board spares, only normal safety equipment and a paddle to get you to shore.

Strictly speaking, on-board spares are not properly a part of a PPM program. Spares of this nature will be used only when a failure has occurred, and this is *corrective* maintenance. Yet, the ready availability of on-board spares makes you less dependent upon others to get you safely home.

In composing this suggested list of on-board spares and how to stow them, we are further guided by the experienced realization that small craft have limited storage space and resources for maintaining a heavy load of spares and materials.

THE BOAT BOX OR "POSSIBLES BOX"

In pioneer days, the possibles box contained many small items that could be used to fabricate almost anything that could not be done without. On small craft it is perhaps better known as the boat box, but it has the same function. It contains as many small things as we can think of to cover all sorts of possibilities.

A plastic fishing tackle box makes an outstanding boat box. It won't rust, has convenient compartments to aid organization, and is easy to stow. A particularly handy skipper creates his own materials, etc. It may still be possible to find government surplus ammunition boxes which, when given added coats of rust-inhibiting paint, make good boat boxes. Putting together a good boat box is a great off-season project for the small craft skipper.

Electrical Spares And Materials

Let us begin with small electrical spares, for nothing will disable an engine more quickly than an electrical failure. If you have an owner's manual or shop manual, there should be an electrical diagram included. On this diagram locate and identify the fuses that the engine requires to protect various circuits against overloads. While not a part of the engine, lighting and equipment fuses should be included. It is not necessary to carry a spare for each fuse. Select a small assortment that will cover the range of all the fuses. For the most part the fuses used on small craft are automotive glass buss fuses. In addition, most of them, because of the low voltage and high current ratings, will be large in ampere current ratings. These fuses can be kept either in the little flat cans they come in, or, better yet, in plastic 35mm film cartridge cans. Used film cans are available at most camera shops. The airtight snap-on covers will keep the fuses separate and insulated from corroding salt air. Label the cans with tape.

Make a survey of the lamp bulbs used aboard for the legally required running lights. Since these lamps are required by Coast Guard regulations, be sure to carry a couple of spares. Usually one or two types of spare lamps (one each) will be sufficient. Also consider carrying a spare bulb for the compass and engine indicating instruments. A spare for the on-board emergency flashlight or electric lantern is also a wise choice. These small items, like the fuses, can be kept in small, labeled plastic cans.

Although they leave much to be desired as marine electrical connectors (because of corrosion problems), a small collection of various sizes and types of crimp-on electrical terminals are useful aboard small craft. (The matching tool to be used with these lugs is carried in the tool box.)

Spare hook-up wire is very useful. A few feet of multi-stranded, medium gauge, insulated wire should do nicely. Small

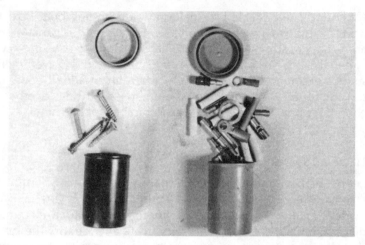

Fig. 4.1   These 35mm film cans make great small parts storage organizers.

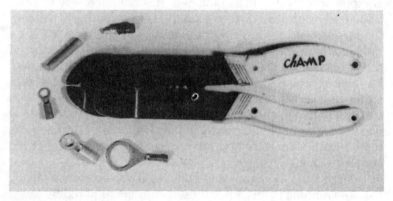

Fig. 4.2   Crimp-type electrical terminals and crimping tool.

spools can be obtained in almost any automotive supply store. Perhaps a few feet of light and extra heavy gauge wire wound on the same spool would be even better. As a general rule, when making an emergency connection always use a wire *equal* to or *heavier* than the wire you are splicing, because the current it must carry might cause a lighter gauge wire to overheat.

Few things in the boat box have more use than a spool of electrician's plastic insulating tape, so be sure to add this to the electrical spares.

You might be wise to make up a several-foot-long jumper wire with either terminal lugs or, better yet, heavy clips on each end. This will be handy if a quick emergency connection is ever needed. A bit of crocus cloth for cleaning and burnishing connections and a small tube of Vaseline for keeping the air from electrical connections are useful. A spray can of insulating drier such as WD40 or any of the many silicone-based products will be helpful.

Cooling System Spares

In Chapter 1 we described one of the tricks of the trade—a small easily stored emergency coolant hose repair kit. This kit will cover all but the most catastrophic cooling system problems involving the hoses. However, if your coolant and exhaust systems use large diameter, molded-to-fit hoses, the kit will not help. These systems rarely give trouble but you might want to carry a single spare. If you have a regular inboard marine engine that is essentially a converted automobile engine (usually the case), consider buying a cheap rebuilt automobile recirculating pump (available in many automotive parts stores for under $15). This pump, while not specifically a marine version, will get you home if the main circulating pump on the engine should fail. Before storing it aboard, give it a light coating of grease or Vaseline and stow it in an airtight plastic bag in any convenient out-of-the-way location.

When you inspect the pump/alternator drive belt, take it completely off of the engine so that you can carefully examine the inside as well as the outside. At this time either measure the overall diameter of the belt or get the part number from the belt itself or from the owner's manual. Keep a spare belt aboard at all times since they do wear out and break, leaving you dead in the water with an overheated engine and an alternator that cannot charge the battery. Some engines use double belts, in which case only one need be carried since the likelihood of both belts breaking at the same time is remote. However, if the engine uses belts of different sizes, carry a spare for each.

Spare hoses can be carried if you find room for them, but with the emergency repair kit aboard it is not necessary. We do not recommend carrying a spare rubber impeller for the coolant water supply pump unless such a pump is completely separated from the engine and easily accessible. For outboards and outdrives the replacement of the pump impeller is a shoreside activity requiring professional assistance. A spare thermostat is not essential because, should the installed unit hang up either in the open or closed position, you can simply remove it and run the engine temporarily without it till you can get back to the dock.

Fuel System Spares

The nature of the fuel system in most small craft limits what spares can be reasonably carried. Fuel pumps (for the most part sealed units which cannot be repaired) seldom cause total engine failure. If you can afford it, carry an entire fuel pump packaged in an airtight plastic bag. However, if you are one of those fortunate few who still have a fuel pump which can be disassembled so that you can replace a ruptured diaphragm or a broken return spring (the major cause of pump failure), then by all means carry a fuel pump rebuilding kit among the on-board spares. A length of rubber fuel line hose and two stainless steel hose clamps of the screw type will repair most fuel line failures. A couple of bronze fittings for the ends of metal fuel lines are inexpensive and easy to store. A spare fuel line filter cartridge, while not absolutely essential to the operation of the system, will be helpful if the present filter becomes clogged with dirt.

Lubrication Materials

Any small craft engine thrives on well lubricated subsystems and there will be many opportunities during short day trips to give various grease and oil points that little extra shot of lubricant that just might save you a lot of grief later on. None of the following items should be construed as emergency spares. However, we suggest that you carry a small cartridge-loaded grease gun that will fit the grease points on your engine and drive unit. With the gun, keep one or two cartridges loaded with marine type grease. A can of light machine oil and a can of penetrating oil will cover most other lubrication needs. Remember, when you need a drop of oil, the best way is to get it from the dip-stick in the engine if you have an inboard engine. If you have an outboard you will have to rely on the small oil can. A small container of any kind filled with Vaseline will be very handy aboard. A spray can of WD40, which is both a lubricant and an insulation protector, is also useful.

Fig. 4.3 Cartridge-loaded grease gun, oil cans, spray cans, gear oil, and penetrating oil.

Drive Train Spares

The failure of any part in the drive train (including clutches, transmissions, linkage (control) steering, shafting, and propellers) will generally disable the boat. Short of a complete spare drive system, you should make some very careful choices regarding what to carry. If you have an outboard, be sure to have aboard at least a couple of shear pins for the propeller. If you can afford it, a spare prop is always a comfort. Stainless steel cotter pins for the propeller hub might be needed. The preceding also applies to small craft with outdrives. A container of heavy-weight gear oil for the drive unit is a necessity and is handy for other purposes.

Ignition Spares

The small craft ignition system is the primary "soft spot." At the minimum, for inboards, a spare distributor cap, rotor, set of points and condenser should be carried in the boat box. Include one or two sparkplugs and a length of sparkplug wire. Among the lubrication spares we included a can of WD40, which will also help with wet components in the ignition system. Small electrical spares previously suggested will take care of most other ignition problems. For outboards the only practical

Fig. 4.4 "Typical" ignition spares, cap, rotor, point set, and condenser.

on-board spares are a couple of sparkplugs. Make sure they are pre-gapped and ready to install. If you own one of the larger outboard engines that uses a conventional automotive ignition system (distributor), the suggested spares for inboards also apply. In most other cases, there is little that can be done on the boat with outboard engine ignition systems, since the flywheel often must be removed to gain access to the points and condenser.

Test Instruments

No elaborate test instruments need to be carried in the boat box. Most test instruments are delicate and cannot stand the rough treatment they will get aboard a small craft. In any case, the most useful device for locating and identifying electrical problems is the test lamp. This small rugged and inexpensive device will help locate almost any engine problem that you are likely to experience. A small combination volt/ohm/milliammeter is very useful but must be stored with such care that it is best kept safely ashore in the gear locker.

SPARES AND MATERIALS KEPT ASHORE IN THE GEAR LOCKER

A new boat owner should consider establishing a place ashore that is reserved for the storage of boat materials and spare parts. Any old locker or a set of shelves in the garage or cellar will do.

In the gear locker keep the oils, greases, and other lubricants occasionally needed for the engine and boat (*in addition to* the similar products carried in the boat box). Also keep a tray of engine fasteners such as bolts, nuts, washers (both flat and lock), and machine screws that are always needed during PPM programs. (Never put a rusted and corroded fastener back on the engine if you can help it. It is bound to fail at the most crucial moment!) Fasteners can be accumulated over a period of time, and we are not suggesting that you rush out and buy a complete collection immediately. Stay with the best quality (stainless steel, silicone bronze) you can afford, and avoid the inexpensive low grade steel and galvanized or brass fasteners that do not have the holding power or the ability to withstand the marine environment.

Lay in a stock of precut gaskets for those most often maintained points on the engine, such as the manifold, thermostat housings, water pumps, and valve case covers. If the pre-cuts seem too expensive, then keep on hand a sheet or two of gasket paper and gasket sealer compound for cutting your own gaskets as described in Chapter 3.

Most modern engines use an extensive number of rubber "O" rings to seal and prevent leaks. If you have a supply of these rings in your locker, you won't have to go chasing for them during a maintenance task. Most of the common sizes are described in your engine maintenance manual. Never try to reuse an "O" ring—always replace it.

The electrical needs that are not carried in the boat box—such as heavy cable, hookup wire, fuses, lamps, fittings, insulating tape, and shrink tubing—should be acquired one by one and kept in the shore-side gear locker.

Also stock up on such items as fuel conditioners or additives. Filters for oil and fuel, bilge cleaners, head treatments, etc., can be picked up during sales and stored in the gear locker for use in your PPM program.

Special Tools And Instruments

The following special tools and instruments are both useful and pay for themselves many times over in a PPM program. Like all previous suggestions they are optional, and each skipper should decide for himself just how independent he wants to be. We have chosen each of the items with the view that they must pay for themselves within one or two seasons of use. Tools and

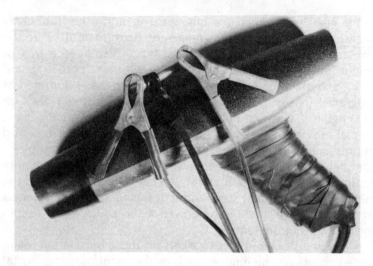

Fig. 4.5 Shown is a DC-powered Xenon timing light. Extra rubber tape on handle for those damp days.

instruments that do not meet this criteria can be borrowed or rented to do a specific maintenance task.

We recommend that you acquire a nonprofessional, DC-powered *timing light*, which can be found in most department stores and mail order catalogs. While less rugged and far less costly than professional lights, they will do nicely for your personal use of two or three times a year. After two do-it-yourself tune-ups on either the boat or car, the light has paid for itself.

To back up the timing light you will need an inexpensive combination *dwell/tachometer*. Again, this item is readily available to the do-it-yourselfer and will do nicely for other than everyday use.

An engine *compression gauge* is very useful for collecting valuable information on engine performance and needs.

Flat feeler gauges and *sparkplug gauges* are needed for engine tune-ups and many other critical adjustments on the engine. These are inexpensive and can be used for the boat or family car.

Skippers with outboard engines will need a *wheel puller*. With this device you can do your own tune-ups. The type suggested has many uses and will fit a large number of pulleys

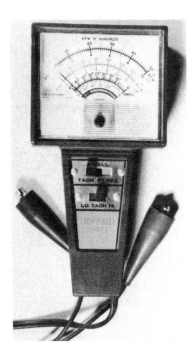

Fig. 4.7   Compression gauges.

Fig. 4.6   Shown here a combination Dwell, Tachometer, and Point Resistance meter.

Fig. 4.8   Feeler gauge set—round for spark plugs and flat for points.

Fig. 4.9   A universal-type wheel gear puller.

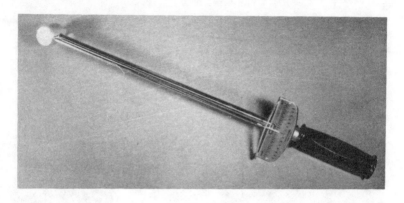

Fig. 4.10   Low-cost torque wrench with drive for *your* socket set.

and wheels that are tightly fitted to drive shafts. The wheel puller is the only thing that will get them off properly.

The modern inboard or outboard engine requires a number of adjustments in which fasteners must be tightened (torqued) to specific foot-pounds settings. Engine manufacturers consider these settings critical and specify the amounts in the engine shop manual. The special *wrenches* to accomplish these adjustments, once available only to the professional, can be purchased from almost any tool supply house. An excellent model, available from a mail order store, will cover the majority of torque foot-pound adjustments on your engine. Use the sockets from your regular socket set to fit any nuts and bolts. Just make sure the socket drive size is the same for each tool.

An inexpensive *specific gravity meter* will tell you far in advance how things are going inside the battery. In addition, the combination AC/DC volt/ohm/milliammeter mentioned previously has so many uses on the boat and around the house and car that it will easily pay for itself in short order. A very good unit sells for well under $20 in an electronic supply store.

If you decide to do your own oil and filter changes you will need an *oil filter strap wrench*. There are many different styles and most of them are quite inexpensive. Like most of the special tools recommended, do not opt for the professional level wrench. A punch-type oil can *spout* is inexpensive and reduces the mess when you are changing the oil in the boat or car.

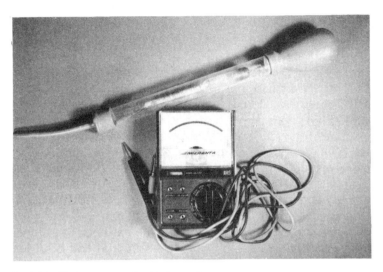

Fig. 4.11   Hydrometer and volt-ohmmeter.

SAFETY AND MONITORING EQUIPMENT

Fire Prevention and Detection Devices

The first line of defense against fire is having *fire extinguishers* where they are most likely to be needed—in the engine area and galley, where fuel is present. The PPM skipper will keep in mind that his fire-fighting equipment is constantly exposed to vibration and moisture and make sure that all extinguishers are frequently tested and maintained according to instructions.

Keep in mind when you are planning and maintaining your boat's safety system that one cup of gasoline in vapor form has the explosive power of *fifteen* sticks of dynamite. (The Coast Guard says that few boats really burn—they explode first, then burn.) Gasoline fumes are heavier than air and accumulate in low areas in the bottom of the boat. A stray spark from a poor and unprotected electrical connection can ignite the fumes. A fire extinguisher cannot prevent an explosion.

There are several devices to detect the presence of gasoline fumes. Two are infallible and never fail when they are utilized. Fortunately for us, vaporized gasoline in the smallest amounts, has a strong odor and is easily detected by sniffing. In spite of opposition from the Coast Guard, Butane and Propane cooking gases are fast becoming popular on small craft. These gases, like gasoline fumes, are heavier than air and will lurk in low places awaiting an ignition spark. Again, and fortunately, they emit an acrid odor that aids in detecting leaks and dangerous conditions. Most gasoline fires and explosions seem to occur shortly after or during fueling, and this is when the common-sense protective device is most reliable. The proper procedures for fueling a boat are a matter of record with the Coast Guard and other boating safety organizations. Free fueling instructions, pamphlets, and instruction sheets are available to any small craft owner.

There are available various electronic *detectors* that react to the presence of dangerous levels of fumes and/or smoke. These units are expensive, and their value has been questioned by some authorities. The human nose is built-in and is far less fallible.

Any small craft with an inboard engine should be protected with added ventilation from a *bilge blower,* an electrically driven fan, usually of the so-called squirrel cage type. The motor that drives the fan must be vaporproof and of the best quality. Although these sealed units require little maintenance, they should be included on PPM inspection lists.

The best protection against the accumulation of explosive fumes in small craft is an active and effective ventilation system for *all* of the low areas in the boat. This system must be carefully maintained at all times.

Federal law requires that two other items of a protective nature aboard small craft with inboard gasoline engines—these are the *backfire flame arrester* and the *carburetor drip pan*. Both devices require periodic and simple preventive maintenance.

The flame arrester is mounted on the top of the air intake throat of the carburetor and is constructed of a series of fine baffles that allow air to be drawn into the engine easily but prevent an open flame (as in the case of an engine backfire) from escaping into the open engine compartment. All air being drawn into the engine contains greasy dust, dirt, and lint that collect on the filter baffles of the flame arrester and act as an unwanted choke on the engine. Obviously, this choking will cause the engine to use more fuel than necessary and to smoke excessively. The greasy deposits badly affect engine sparkplugs and result in general poorer performance. To properly clean the flame arrester, remove it from the engine and give it a thorough bath, either in a degreasing tank at the local filling station or in

Fig. 4.12 Bilge blower fan, squirrel cage type.

Fig. 4.13 Backfire flame arrester for up-draft carburetors. (*Note:* This design does not require a drip pan.)

a strong detergent and water solution. Rinse it several times in clear water and blow it dry with compressed air or with a hair dryer. A light rinse with alcohol will accelerate the drying. Do not wash the flame arrester in gasoline. For a quick treatment with the flame arrester mounted on the engine, a spray can of engine degreaser together with vigorous brushing and wiping will cure a dirt problem *temporarily,* but a full scrubbing is called for at the earliest practical moment.

Some older marine engines in small craft use side- or up-draft carburetors. These carburetors are protected with flame arresters that, while different in appearance, function in the same manner and require the same cleaning maintenance. In addition, up-draft carburetors are required to have a gasoline *drip pan* installed under the carburetor to catch and hold any gasoline that drips from the carburetor. A suspicious and careful eye should be kept on the contents of the drip pan.

Finally, many modern inboard marine engines vent hot oily fumes from the valve case covers by means of hoses from the covers to the flame arrester. These oil wastes cause further dirt accumulation problems on the flame arrester. To rid them of accumulated greasy gunk, the hoses should be punched out periodically and washed thoroughly.

We recommend that skippers whose small craft engines are installed beneath an engine box consider installing (if you don't already have one) an opening in the engine box cover, large enough to admit the nozzle of a fire extinguisher. The hole can be cut with a sabre saw or with a hole saw chucked into an electric drill. A heavy flap can be installed on the inside of the hole to keep out unwanted moisture. In case of fire, an extinguisher can be discharged through the hole and into the engine area *without* opening the engine box, which invariably admits more oxygen to feed the flame and exposes the fire fighter to bad flash burns. A hole in the engine box cover may soon become a federal requirement.

Automatic Bilge Alarms

All small craft should have some device for removing excess water from the bilge. Small boats can be bailed with a large bucket or a scoop made from a plastic bleach water jug. Larger boats can be bailed with a reliable and inexpensive hand-operated pump. If your boat is equipped with automatic, electrically operated bilge pumps, however, remember that any pump's capacity to pump water *out* of the boat is limited, and if the water coming in exceeds the rate at which the bilge pump is able to discharge it, a potentially dangerous and embarrassing condition can rapidly develop. As a hedge against this possibility, consider installing an automatic high water level bilge alarm. All you need to fabricate and install your own warning system is a float switch (such as a glass-enclosed mercury switch) connected mechanically to a float arm, and either an audio or visual indicator such as a lamp or buzzer. All of these components are readily available at electronic supply stores, and many are designed for 12-volt DC operation.

Fig. 4.14   A home made automatic bilge water level float switch (float material yet to be trimmed to size).

electronic supply stores, and many are designed for 12-volt DC operation.

Engine Performance Monitoring Systems

Engine performance monitoring systems are designed to signal the onset of problems in the engine *before* they reach the catastrophe point. In addition to the previously described engine use-time meters, there are several other types of monitors, some of which you may want to install on your boat. For the most part, these monitoring devices and their associated pick-ups or "senders" require little preventive maintenance other than a periodic inspection and cleaning of electrical contacts and terminal lugs.

Electrical [Current and Voltage]   "Idiot lights" do not warn of potential trouble—they only indicate that something has already failed. If you have one of these devices on your boat, we recommend that you install an *indicating ammeter* for the engine charging system at your earliest convenience. Installation is not difficult, and the wire presently used to light the lamp can be used. A superior installation includes a monitoring voltmeter that, together with the ampmeter, will not only monitor charge and discharge to and from the battery but also indicate the level at which it is taking place. Voltmeters are

Fig. 4.15   Example of a small craft ammeter.

Fig. 4.16   Example of a small craft temperature gauge.

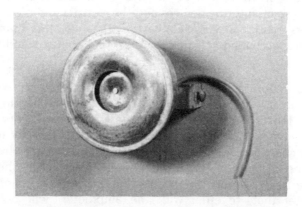

Fig. 4.17   Small, inexpensive audio buzzer (12 volts DC) ideal as audio warning device for small craft.

more sensitive to changes in circuit conditions and can predict upcoming troubles before they get serious.

Overtemperature [Coolant and Lubrication Oil]   It is important to monitor the temperature of engine coolant, lubrication oil and drive unit lubrication. The latter two normally are reserved for larger boats, but it is helpful to monitor these crucial temperatures on any inboard engine and drive unit. (Outboards are of course excluded from oil temperature monitoring as the lubrication oil is mixed with the fuel.)

In many cases boats are equipped with automotive indicator lights, even for something as important as coolant temperature. Because these burned out monitoring lamps do not indicate (except when the ignition key is first turned on), the engine can overheat, seize up and be ruined. Let us again emphasize that because the marine engine, when in gear, is always under a strain, it is important to monitor internal conditions. The coolant overtemperature warning lamp, usually red, should catch the attention of the operator immediately. However, the value of the lamp is limited if the pilot's attention is more properly occupied maintaining a good lookout all around the boat as it is proceeding through the water. The best overtemperature warning system for coolants includes an audible buzzer that is activated simultaneously with the warning lamp. The installation is simple and inexpensive. A small 12-volt DC buzzer can be purchased at any electronic parts supply store for less than $2 and connected across the warning lamp in parallel, on the back of the instrument panel. For small craft this system is adequate.

A temperature gauge is preferred by many skippers and will better indicate the temperature of the coolant from second to second. A problem will be indicated by a rise in temperature *before* it becomes critical. The value of the gauge is limited by the skipper's instrument scanning habits while the boat is underway. If you have a warning light for coolant overtemperature, you can easily install a temperature gauge in place of the lamp. The sensor or sender is a thermally activated switch and will have to be changed at the engine. Thus a change of temperature is converted to an equivalent change in electric current. This, in turn, causes a needle indication on the face of the meter. (This arrangement will not do for a meter that requires a sensor that changes its resistance in direct proportion to a change in temperature.)

Fig. 4.18   Example of engine oil pressure gauge for small craft.

It is often useful to monitor the operating temperature of the lubricating oil in high-performance engines, and, in addition to keep an eye on the oil pressure. Oil temperatures can easily reach critical points in these engines, and often a separate oil cooling system is required. For the most part, however, this will only concern the skipper who races his small craft.

Manifold Air Pressure   Although we have never seen one, there may be a stock boat that comes equipped with a manifold air pressure gauge (or vacuum gauge). At one time such gauges were used in the final steps of tuning an engine. In order to bring an engine to peak performance after setting time and dwell, the air pressure must be adjusted to any optimum specified level by adjusting the carburetor. However, the term *air pressure* can be misleading. The pressure in the intake manifold of a four-cycle gasoline engine is said to be negative—that is, it is *less* than the atmospheric pressure outside the engine. The skipper who wishes to obtain optimum performance at the lowest fuel cost will find that a vacuum gauge, together with a tachometer, will do a better than adequate job. The vacuum gauge, mounted in the dash at the operator's position, provides instantaneous and accurate indications of engine performance. In addition, this gauge will also display data that is predictive, and an operator who is

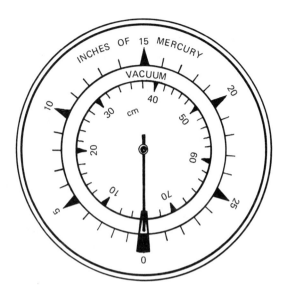

Fig. 4.19 Manifold air pressure gauge that can be used on small craft.

Fig. 4.20 Small craft fuel flow meters. (Photo courtesy of FloScan Instrument Co.)

minimally skilled at reading this data should be able to diagnose the problem. Installing the gauge is not difficult. Most engines have a blanked-off plug in the manifold. The plug can be removed and a hose adapter screwed into the threaded plug hole. A hose can be connected tightly to the adapter, run up to the operator's position, and connected to the manifold pressure gauge. The interpretations of the readings or indications of these gauges may be found in several do-it-yourself automotive repair books.

Fuel Pressure Gauge and Flow Meter   There can be a few skippers who do not want to increase the propulsion system's efficiency to its maximum; and a fuel flow meter, together with a manifold pressure gauge (or tachometer), will provide the data to accomplish this goal. Bear in mind that this instrumentation *can* be useful but is optional. Engine efficiency can just as easily be achieved and maintained by planned and concientiously carried out preventive maintenance, a gentle hand on the throttle, and a more leisurely attitude toward the time required to get from one boating point to another. A fuel pressure gauge may be thought of as an unnecessary luxury since it will only monitor the output of the fuel pump. On small craft this is not generally considered a crucial bit of data, and the gauge may only serve to clutter up the instrument panel.

Lubrication Oil Pressure Gauge   This monitoring device on all four-cycle engines is *crucial*. There must be an indicator that will warn the operator that there has been a failure in the engine's lubrication system. Most stock small craft with inboard engines come equipped with some sort of an indicator to do this. The most common indicator is the idiot light which comes to us from the automotive field. The light will do the job adequately, but it is more effective if coupled with an audio warning buzzer (such as the one previously suggested for coolant system monitors). An indicator lamp may be easily converted to a direct reading gauge.

The skipper must choose between two types of gauge. One type conveys a sample of the oil pressure all the way from the engine pick-up point to the instrument panel through a length of semi-flexible metal tubing. Some danger to the tubing results from careless installation (sharp bends). The tubing is also vulnerable to galvanic attack, vibration, and loose connections. Any leak or fracture in the tubing causes hot black oil to spray all over everything. The electrical type of meter is not subject to these potential hazards. However, the sender or pickup in the engine (as in the case of the coolant temperature conversion) must be changed from a simple thermally operated switch to a pressure-sensitive, variable-resistance pickup. A change in oil pressure causes an equivalent change in resistance in the pickup, and a corresponding change in electric current is then shown on the meter or gauge.

Most of the meters, gauges, and other warning and indicating devices may be obtained from marine hardware stores or automotive supply stores. Installation of the gauge or meter is simplified by the use of a hole saw inserted into an ordinary drill to make a perfect round hole in the mounting panel.

Tachometer   The tachometer is one of the very best of all the engine performance monitoring instruments. This device, which normally reads engine revolutions per minute (RPM), can also be adapted for use as a navigational and piloting device simply by the construction of a table or chart of RPM versus a known or measured distance. Such a table will indicate the speed over ground, which is of more interest to the pilot than speed through the water. There are several instruments that indicate speed through the water but many are unable to compensate for the effect of current going with or against the boat. Thus there are inherent inaccuracies in these instruments.

The construction of a speed-over-ground table requires that you run your boat over a measured distance course at various throttle settings for a series of RPM settings. A measured mile course can be found on many marine charts, and when these are not available two fixed on-shore objects whose distance apart is known can be used. If there is wind or current present, each run must be made with and against these forces and the results averaged. The boat's load (fuel, passengers, gear) must be listed on the chart and a note taken on the bottom hull condition. Using graph paper, put the throttle settings on the horizontal line and on the vertical line note the speed over the measured distance (timed by a stop watch or a watch with a sweep second hand). The first run between the two points is made at a throttle setting of RPM that closely approximates the speed of five knots (as an example). Note the time required to run the distance. A second run in the opposite direction will give more accurate results when the two are averaged. The arithmetic needed to plot points on the chart for each run is no more complex than multiplying the distance (which is known) by 60 and dividing this result by the time (in minutes). Take a number of observations in runs of RPM increments. Plot each run as a dot on the chart and then connect the dots with a soft curve. From this speed curve you can construct a more easily used table of speed for a given RPM setting. One word of caution: If the two fixed and measured points that you are running between are measured as a nautical mile, your speed will be in *knots* (not knots per hour—just knots). If the distance is in statute miles, your speed will be expressed in miles per hour. Because of the factors mentioned, the speed through the water can be wildly misleading and should not be used for any kind of accurate piloting. The carefully plotted speed curve is much more accurate if small variants such as wind, current, and load are calculated in your future piloting.

Obviously, the tachometer is primarily useful for piloting. However, it does monitor the engine RPM, an essential bit of data when monitoring engine performance. The tachometer also detects and displays small changes that the ear cannot. A gradual drop in RPM over a period of time might indicate that it is time for a tune-up, that the hull is fouled, that the boat is overloaded, etc. Most modern tachometers are electrical, although a few of the mechanical cable-driven types might still be around. Some of the electrical types are noisy and interfere with boat radios. With the advent of integrated circuits and the light emitting diodes (LEDs) we expect to see many digital read-out tachometers on small craft soon. The modern electrical tachometer is essentially a counting device which, when connected to the low-voltage side of the distributor, counts the number of pulses coming from the point set. Through its circuitry it divides the pulses by the number of cylinders in the engine and displays the results as engine revolutions per minute.

The data that can be collected from all of these monitoring devices is essential to a well planned PPM program. Generally, a good and well carried out inspection system will provide a

HOW TO GRAPH YOUR SPEED

Pick a day when the water surface is still and the wind is as light as possible. Over a measured mile course or between well defined and accurately-measured marks, make a series of runs at different rpm settings. Reverse direction and repeat each run in the opposite direction. Average the stopwatch time for the two runs to compensate for current or wind then find speed from the tables. Plot five or six speeds then draw a smooth curve through the points. Use this curve for computing dead reckoning advance. Using a different color pencil, you can also plot your fuel consumption rate for various speeds on this same graph.

ENGINE RPM/VESSEL SPEED CURVE

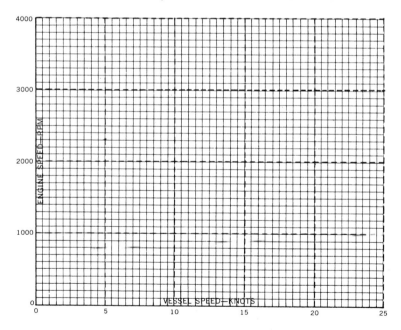

Fig. 4.21   A chart for determining RPM versus speed.

secondary substitute for most of the missing monitoring devices. However, you cannot do without some method of recording engine use time if periodic preventive maintenance is to be carried out in a practical and effective manner.

5
TOOLS AND TEST EQUIPMENT FOR ENGINE PPM

In Chapter 4 we described and listed some suggestions for parts and materials to be carried on board in the boat box. In addition, further suggestions were made for keeping a boat gear locker ashore. We must emphasize again that all of these are suggestions and reminders and that each skipper should decide for himself what suits his boat's needs, the boating environment, and any potential emergency. Much the same applies to the following list of tools and test equipment. There is no question but that tools carried aboard a small craft take a beating—especially if the boat is used in salt water. Tools can be mislaid or loaned and never returned, and they have a tendency to fall overboard. For these reasons, you should carry only those you really need and leave your more expensive tools on shore.

TOOLS

Wrenches

Carry a modest set of box-end wrenches. Much like socket sets, they grip the entire surface area of the nut or stud, and a lot of torque can be applied without danger of the wrench slipping or mangling the fastener. A set of open-end wrenches is also recommended. It is often impossible to get a box-end wrench over the head of a fastener because of nearby fixtures, and the only thing that will fit is an open-end wrench. Both types of wrenches come in a wide variety of styles and sizes. Some have offset handles, others are "S" shaped, and some have 90° bends

Fig. 5.1   A set of box-end wrenches.

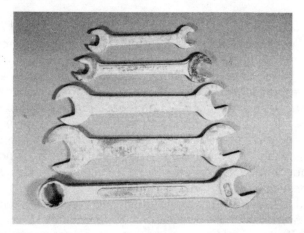

Fig. 5.2   A set of open-end wrenches. Combination wrenches at bottom.

to get at a very awkward nut or bolt. Also available are combination sets in which each size wrench has a box fitting on one end and an open fitting on the other.

An inexpensive foreign-made ratchet and socket set will be useful, although the ratchet is not necessary. A set of Allen wrenches can be used to drive the socket sets, to fit those rare Allen plugs sometimes found on small craft, and to set up or loosen Allen screws. One or two adjustable wrenches may be required, but keep in mind that they often slip as badly as any open-end wrench. Use them only when nothing else will do. A set of nut drivers is handy but not essential. Carry them only if you have the room.

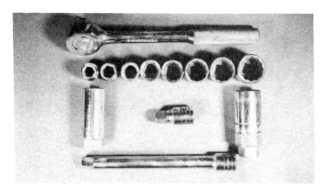

Fig. 5.3 A set of sockets, drive extenders, and spark plug sockets.

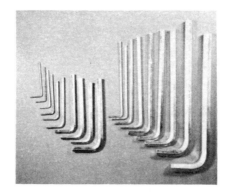

Fig. 5.4 A set of Allen wrenches.

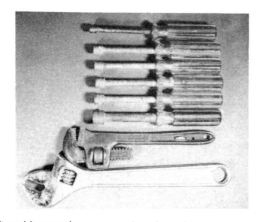

Fig. 5.5 Adjustable wrench, pipe wrench and nut-driver set.

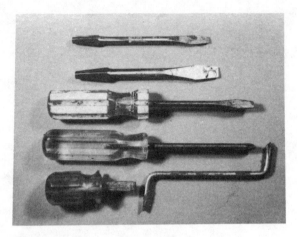

Fig. 5.6 Types of screwdrivers: two bit and brace blades, a standard and a stubby flat blade, a Phillips head, and an offset.

Screwdrivers

Screwdrivers are among the most often used (and misused) tools aboard small craft. You should carry a set of flat blades in three sizes and at least two of the Phillips type in two sizes. There are sets of screwdrivers with one drive handle and various sizes of blades and lengths of shafts that will conserve storage space in the tool box. One of the more useful types of screwdriver is that designed to be chucked in a bit brace so that the greatest amount of torque can be applied. (In fact, you must be careful not to shear off the fastener from the head.) This tool is very helpful to release a fastener that has seized up from corrosion and rust.

Gripping Tools

Next to screwdrivers, these are the most often used tools. A hefty pair of gas pliers will do most jobs, but a pair of adjustable water pump pliers are equally as useful. Needle-nose pliers are needed for electrical work and for getting small parts started on threads. Vise-grip pliers have almost unlimited uses—for example, they can be used as clamps to hold anything being glued or, in an emergency, temporarily to hold parts together. They also can be used as a vise to hold a part being sawed or filed. Used as designed they will grip a frozen fastener with teeth and extra

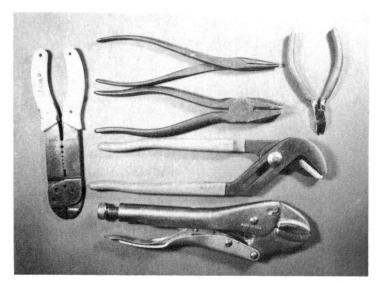

Fig. 5.7 Water pump pliers, lineman's pliers, needle nose pliers, small diagonal cutters, vise grips, and crimping tool.

pressure that, while it might destroy the fastener, will get it loose.

Hammer

The hammer is an optional tool, for it is seldom needed on small craft. However, you *never* should use another tool to hammer with unless you are prepared to replace it. Around engines the ball peen hammer is best. It need not be large or heavy, and the handle should be short for easy storage.

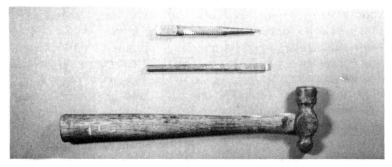

Fig. 5.8 Hammer, ball peen, cold chisel, and metal punch.

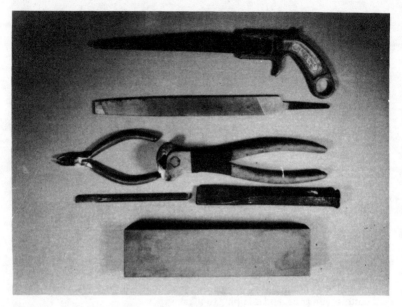

Fig. 5.9 Types of cutting tools: small hacksaw, file, nippers, chisel, and sharpening stone.

Cutting Tools

Almost all of the following cutting tools are optional, but their usefulness, provided there is room for them, cannot be denied. A hacksaw (one that does not require a complete frame to hold the blade) with extra interchangeable blades will be enough for most requirements. A pair of diagonal cutters is often needed but a combination tool (such as the crimping tool) can be used. This tool crimps terminal lugs to wire, strips the insulation from various sizes of wire, and cuts wire. Some have various sized threaded holes for cutting small machine screws. Heavy nippers are useful for shearing off protruding nails or screws and for pulling out fasteners. At least one chisel for cutting metal may be needed and requires little space in the tool box. A set of mill files, including one flat and one half-round, and a round rasp have their place. Something on the boat always is in need of a new sharp edge which can be shaped with the file and finished with an oil stone. A small oil stone is essential to keep all bladed tools sharp. A jackknife (including the Boy Scout variety) has as many uses as a screwdriver and should be kept in the tool box.

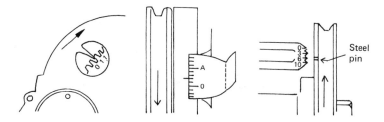

Fig. 5.10 Timing marks on a pulley (vibration damper) and engine block in coincidence.

Space Gauges

Space or "feeler" gauges are required around engines of any kind but especially small craft. Most come in sets and are inexpensive and easy to carry aboard in the tool box. Round gauges are used to set the gap of the electrodes on spark plugs, and flat gauges are used to set the gap between the point contacts of the distributor (also called *dwell*) and to set the spacing of valve tappets. (Many modern inboard engines use hydraulic valve lifters and spacing is set without the need of a spacing gauge.) All other critical space settings within the engine are better left to a professional mechanic.

TEST INSTRUMENTS

Test Lamp

There are several test instruments that *could* be carried in the tool box, but if we apply the criteria of usefulness, ruggedness, and low cost, all but one or two devices are eliminated. The test lamp mentioned earlier has all of the characteristics of the limiting criteria above. In the hands of an inspired improviser, this little gadget will locate and identify most electrical problems in and around an engine as well as any light equipment electrical supply problems. True, it is little more than a continuity tester, but on small craft, where the voltage supply is normally 12 volts DC, the test lamp is the fastest and easiest device to use for finding an open, shorted, or complete circuit.

There are a few special applications for the versatile test lamp. For example, to set time on the engine, rotate the engine (using a bump switch) until the number one cylinder is at top dead center (as indicated by the marks on the idler pulley and

Fig. 5.11   Feeler gauges.

the timing marks on the engine block, usually on the front of the engine). Connect the test lamp to the terminal post on the coil of the wire that comes from the distributor (points). Loosen timing adjust clamping bolt on the base of the distributor assembly just enough to barely allow the entire distributor assembly to be turned by hand. Energize the ignition system with the ignition key to the ON position. If the engine is slightly out of time the lamp will be on. To adjust the timing, grasp the distributor with both hands and turn the entire assembly in the direction indicated in the engine manual. Stop *just* at the point where the lamp goes out, which for most engines is the proper place to time the engine. However, most of the modern engines have been designed to operate at a substantial advance in timing. This will be indicated by the timing marks on the idler pulley and engine block. Set these two marks in coincidence with the bump switch and proceed as before. Once you have set the distributor in the timed position, retighten the clamp bolt at the base of the distributor, making sure that the distributor setting is not changed as you tighten the clamp.

This method of timing the engine may be thought of as static as opposed to the dynamic method, which requires the use of a timing light. When done with reasonable care, the static method is quite satisfactory and will be as accurate as the dynamic method.

Should you elect (as we hope you will) to do your own tune-ups, keep in mind that the "dwell" of the points or the spacing of the gap between the point contacts must be adjusted *before* you set the time. Dwell will affect the time but not the other way around.

Fig. 5.12   Audio continuity tester.

Audio Continuity Checker

This little device is recommended as an alternate to the test lamp. It has one or two advantages over the test lamp that may be debatable, but that is left for each skipper to decide. Essentially, the device is nothing more than a small portable audio-oscillator powered by a transistor battery. When the two leads of the tester are connected to a complete (but unpowered) electrical circuit, the continuity of the electrical circuit is indicated by a shrill audio note or buzz from the device. Thus, it has the advantage over the lamp in that continuity is indicated by sound rather than a light that must be constantly viewed by the operator. If the circuit under test contains resistance, the audio note will be higher in frequency. The lamp *might* indicate resistance by dimming, but that change is not as readily detected as a change in audio frequency. Unlike the lamp, which must be used on "hot" (power applied) circuits, the audio checker must be used on "cold" circuits with the power off. Depending on circumstances, there is an advantage to either feature.

SPECIAL TEST EQUIPMENT

In the following paragraphs we will describe and recommend several special test instruments that will be of substantial use to the PPM skipper. These instruments, once the exclusive property of the professional mechanic, are now available at a reasonable price to anyone. Each instrument has been chosen with the view that it must pay for itself after two or three uses. For example, a thorough engine tune-up can cost up to $50. Thus, if you do one or two tune-ups per year yourself, the instruments used quickly pay for themselves. Best of all, you may find that you can also tune up your car, and then the instruments begin to make a profit. We recommend that you purchase nonprofessional-quality instruments—that is, instruments that are accurate but not of the super-rugged construction required for everyday use in a busy professional repair shop. Nonprofessional test instruments are available in many department stores, in electronic supply stores, and sometimes in automotive supply stores, where the more costly professional instruments are also sold.

Combination Dwell-Point Resistance Tachometer

This device will allow you to install and adjust point sets in a distributor dynamically, set carburetor idle and needle valve adjustments, and observe engine RPM right at the engine. It is suitable for use on both two-cycle outboards and four-cycle inboards. Switches allow you to select four-, six-, or eight-cylinder engines and to select what the meter is to read out. When a new set of points and the associated new condenser have been installed, this instrument will be able to complete the following tests: point resistance and adjustment, cam dwell angle and adjustment, and distributor centrifugal advance test (no adjustment). In addition, by means of a cylinder balance test, the instrument can tell you if any cylinder is weaker than the rest. It will provide a test for the air-to-fuel ratio of the carburetor and will test the back-fire flame arrester for proper air capacity. Finally, the instrument provides the necessary read-out (by the tachometer) to adjust the idle-speed screw and idle-mixture screws on the carburetor. Obviously, such an instrument is not only versatile but will allow you to collect factual data on engine condition and performance for your PPM plan. In the chapter to follow we will detail each of these tests step-by-step.

Timing Lights

There are two types of timing lights available to the PPM skipper. An inexpensive neon lamp can be purchased for under $50. Its main disadvantage is that, because the power for the lamp comes only from spark plug voltage, the light emitted by the lamp is too weak to be seen in bright light. If you use this lamp in the evening, however, it is as accurate as the most expensive professional model. A better timing light, which should be just right for PPM skippers, is powered by the battery plus the spark plug voltage. One of the more elaborate lamps requires 120 volts of AC to power the light as well as the spark plug voltage. In addition, the pickup lead needs only to be clipped to the plug lead instead of inserted in series. Its advantages, however, are offset by its price.

In addition to setting the engine exactly on time, the timing light can be used to test individual spark plugs and wires for proper operation and to test both the mechanical advance system in the distributor and the automatic vacuum advance system on automobile engines. (Automobile engines that have been converted to marine use may retain the vacuum advance system, but most experts agree that the mechanical automatic advance system is sufficient for the needs of a marine engine.) The timing light can also be used to check the performance of suspected malfunctioning valves.

Compression Gauge

The value of this gauge for gathering engine performance data, its low cost, and its ease of use more than offset its questionable value as a preventive maintenance gadget. With this simple device you can determine the condition of valves, cylinders, rings, and head gaskets and pinpoint trouble spots. For example, you can decide for yourself if the engine is in need of a valve job and not leave the determination either to chance or the honesty of the mechanic.

Battery Hydrometer

This device meets all of the specifications previously listed for small craft PPM tools: It is simple to operate and read, and it costs very little in proportion to its value. Also, it can be used on the family car. There are many more complex instruments, but none will meet more effectively the basic requirements of the do-it-yourself PPM skipper.

6
SMALL CRAFT ENGINE PPM FROM ADUST TO ZERK

In the following paragraphs we will give detailed step-by-step instructions for the preventive maintenance activities designed to get a small craft inboard engine ready for the season and to keep it ready throughout the season. No attempt has been made to suggest a schedule for these activities, that being best left to the individual skipper to integrate in his own personal PPM plan. Each PPM task is evaluated to be well within the capabilities of the average small craft owner. No highly specialized skills, tools, materials, or instruments are required other than those suggested in previous chapters. Each task is described separately so that you can decide what you will do yourself and what you will leave to the professionals. Once you have started you may soon be doing them all. We will begin with easy, more mundane tasks and advance to those that are more complex.

DRAIN AND CHANGE ENGINE OIL AND OIL FILTER
Estimated Savings: $7 to $10

Refer to Chapter 3 where we described several "tricks" for draining and changing engine oil in an inboard gasoline engine.

1. Consult the engine maintenance manual for recommended oil weight for your boating area and engine use. Also identify the oil filter by brand and model number and note alternates. Enter this data in the Engine Use-Time Log. Follow the money-saving suggestions for purchasing lube oil and oil filters (Chapter 3).

2. Start the engine and warm to operating temperature. If the boat is out of the water, use a hose to provide cooling water to the engine.

3. Shut down the engine and drain the old oil using any of the methods suggested in Chapter 3.

4. Remove and discard the old filter.

5. Install the new filter. *Caution: Do not overtighten.*

6. Install the fresh engine oil. Check the dipstick for proper level.

7. Start and warm the engine. Check for leaks around the new filter and tighten as necessary. Stop the engine and recheck the dipstick for proper level.

CHANGE SPARK PLUGS
Estimated Savings on Eight-Cylinder Engine: $5 to $7

1. Consult the engine maintenance manual for recommended brand and type of spark plug and note alternate brand choices. Determine proper gap spacing of electrodes for your engine model. Enter this data in your log.

2. Purchase new spark plugs. (If you use spares, replace them.) Take advantage of sales.

3. Tools: spark plug wrenches (appropriate deep-throat socket and ratchet), spark plug gap gauge, and spark plug thread starter (as suggested in Chapter 3).

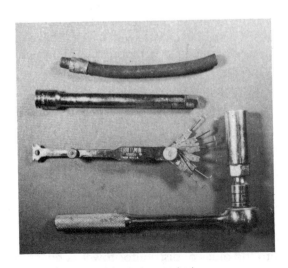

Fig. 6.1   Tools for changing and gapping spark plugs.

4. Loosen all plugs but do not remove them until you have carefully blown the dirt from around the base of the plug. The dirt must not fall into the port or foul the threads for the new plug.

5. Remove the old plugs and "read" them. The condition of old plugs will give much valuable information on engine performance and other settings.

6. Using a gap gauge, set the proper gap as specified in the engine manual.

7. Put a drop or two of oil on the plug threads and start them into their respective holes by *hand. Caution: Do not cross-thread them.*

8. Tighten the plugs to the specifications in the manual (or one-half turn beyond first tighten). *Note:* Many of the new plugs are tapered to make a good seal and do not use compression washers. Thus, the degree of tightness may be given in torque foot pounds. A torque wrench sufficient for your needs can be purchased or rented. Choose one that covers the majority of torque requirements according to the table in the engine manual.

9. Remove and inspect, one at a time, each spark plug high-tension wire. Look for cracks in the insulation, chafe spots, and general condition of the wire. *Note:* Many engines use electronic noise-suppressing resistance-type spark plug wires. As these wires get older, the resistance may increase radically and cause poor performance. Any suspicion should be confirmed by measuring the resistance of each wire with a small inexpensive *ohmmeter.* As a rule, a reading of more than 15,000 ohms means that you should replace the wire at first opportunity.

10. Inspect the wire looms and rubber grommets. Look for chafing where wire passes through the loom. Replace or add new grommets as indicated.

11. Inspect the boots at both ends of wire, looking for burns, cracks or any signs of reduced insulating quality.

12. Inspect the *inside* of the distributor tower connections where the plug wire enters the distributor. Look for signs of corrosion and burnish clean. Blow out before reconnecting the plug wire. Be sure that the plug wires and boots are firmly pressed onto the plugs or distributor tower connectors. Finally, spray the wires with ignition insulating spray such as WD40.

Fig. 6.2   Inspect inside of distributor towers.

CHANGE POINT SET, CONDENSER, ROTOR, AND DISTRIBU-TOR CAP
Estimated Savings: UP TO $25

1. Consult the engine maintenance manual to obtain data on point gap spacing (dwell) and timing (the number of degrees of advance from top dead center, or TDC).

2. Purchase a point set, condenser, rotor, and distributor cap for your engine. (If you use your spares, immediately replace them.)

3. Gather the following tools: a small and a medium size screwdriver, a set of flat feeler gauges, a can of degreasing spray or solvent, a can of light oil, and a small amount of distributor cam grease or a new cam lubricating wick.

4. Using a bright light, inspect the outside top of the distributor cap for dirt and grease, salt deposits, cracks, and carbon tracks. If you decide to replace the distributor cap, hold the new cap close to the old cap and position both caps the same. Replace the spark plug wires by transferring them one at a time so as not to get connections crossed. If the old cap is to be retained, carefully wash the outside with a solvent and dry with clean cloth or paper towel.

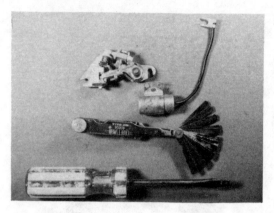

Fig. 6.3   Point-changing tools.

5. Release the distributor cap hold-down clamps. On some distributors these are spring-loaded "J" clamps that can be released by pressing and turning with a screwdriver. On others there are small machine screws. Consider replacing rusted or corroded hold-down screws. Remove the distributor cap from the distributor body and, using a strong light, carefully inspect the inside of the cap for cracks, carbon tracks, signs of moisture, and wear at the button contact in the center of the cap and at individual plug wire contacts around the perimeter. Wash with solvent and carefully dry with cloth or paper towel. *Note:* Inspection of the inside of the cap often reveals upcoming troubles due to distributor shaft wear and rotor malfunction. Consider replacing a distributor cap that shows any signs of wear or cracks.

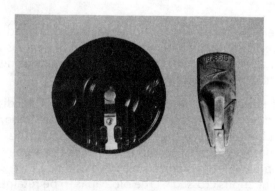

Fig. 6.4   Examples of distributor rotors. (Round is G.M.)

Fig. 6.5 Checking rotor for correct size against inside of cap. Note small gap between rotor tip and cap electrode.

6. Remove the distributor rotor by pulling the rotor straight up from the distributor shaft. (Some rotors may be held in place with screws, which must be removed and carefully set aside for re-use.)

7. Inspect the rotor for cracks, corrosion, or carbon at the metal tip. Burnish the rotor and set it aside as a spare, or discard and replace it. Be sure that the rotor to be installed is the proper size to match the distributor cap. Place the rotor inside the cap, noting the spacing between the rotor electrode and any one of the sparkplug wire electrodes. The electrodes should be very close but not touching when the rotor is centered in the cap.

8. Inspect the mechanical advance weights for signs of rust and corrosion. (The advance weights are just under the rotor or under the distributor point set plate.) Clean and burnish as indicated and *lightly* oil. Look for broken springs but do not remove unless they are to be replaced. If you have suspicions about the mechanical advance weights, call in a professional mechanic.

9. Loosen and remove the leads (wires) from the point set to the condenser and to the coil. (These wires are held in place with either a screw or a spring-loaded clip.) For the moment, dress the leads out of the way.

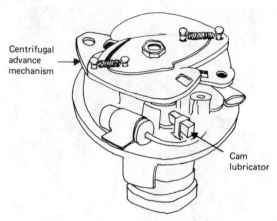

Fig. 6.6   Topside mechanical advance weights.

Fig. 6.7   Condenser lead on point set connector block.

10. Loosen the condenser clamp retainer screw and remove the condenser. (*Note*: If a clamp has not been provided with the new condenser , purchase one separately. Discard the old clamp—its condition connot be precisely determined without sophisticated electronic test equipment.) Install the new condenser under the clamp and tighten the clamp screw. Temporarily dress the lead wire of the condenser out of the way.

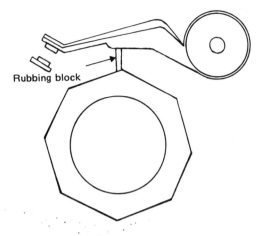

Rubbing block

Fig. 6.8   Rubbing block on a cam-high point.

11. Study the point set assembly for a moment. Some point sets are held in place with one or two clamp screws. Some point sets are adjusted by means of an eccentric head screw that stays in the mounting plate, not in the point set, others are adjusted by means of a simple screwdriver. Loosen and remove the point set clamp screw and set it aside—you may need it later. When the point set has been removed, inspect the contact faces. Burned, heavily pitted surfaces on the points indicate troubles elsewhere. If there are excessive pits on either side of the point faces, the condenser may be electrically too large or too small. Some points have a hole in the center to help cool the faces of the points.

12. Install the new point set but only finger-tighten the clamp screws—you've yet to set the point space gap. "Bump" or jog the engine over using a jog switch until the point set rubbing block is sitting exactly on any one of the high points on the distributor shaft cam.

13. Select a flat feeler gauge of proper size and insert it between the open faces of the point set. You may have to open the faces up by means of the screw slot adjustment. Adjust the space between the point faces to match as closely as possible the thickness of the flat feeler gauge. When the point set spacing (or

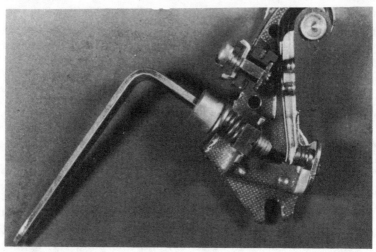

Fig. 6.9   a) Common type: point set adjust clamp screw. Note slot for adjusting space (dwell) just to the right of clamp screw. b) GM is adjusted from outside the distributor.

dwell or cam angle) has been set to specifications, tighten the point set clamp screw. Use care as this often causes the point set to move slightly and change the point set spacing. Check the spacing with a dwell meter after the screw has been tightened.

Fig. 6.10 Set point spacing (dwell) with flat feeler gauge to specs. Shown out of the engine for clarity.

One final word of caution. While point faces can be filed to remove pits and burned faces to get a few more hours of use, this, in effect, removes the special metal facing of the points and only hastens the time when the points must be replaced. So don't file unless there is no other alternative.

14. Inspect the cam grease wick, which usually is a sponge-like bar or doughnut-shaped device that holds a special grease to lubricate the cam and reduce rubbing block wear. It is not recommended that any attempt be made to add grease to the wick. If the wick seems dry, it should be replaced along with the point set and condenser. The doughnut-shaped wicks can be rotated 180° or the bar-shaped wicks can be turned end-for-end for another season of use.

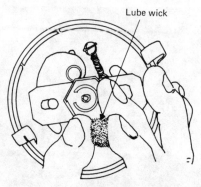

Fig. 6.11   Check the condition of the cam lubricating wick.

Fig. 6.12   Check the condition of the rotor shaft wick (if used).

15. At the top of the distributor shaft (or in a hollow space under the rotor on many distributors) you'll see a small oil pad. This pad should be removed and renewed if it has dried up. If you cannot find a replacement, lightly apply a few drops of light machine oil to the pad and to the top of the distributor shaft.

16. Install the new rotor. (*Note:* Make sure that it is the correct size by setting it inside the cap. Check the spacing at the metal electrode at the end of the rotor and the contacts inside the distributor cap. There should be only enough space to allow the rotor to clear the cap contacts.) After you have installed the

Fig. 6.13   Square (bottom) and round (top) guides (in white) on General Motors-type rotors. These fit in guide holes atop advance weights.

rotor, twist it lightly to make sure it is on the keyway on top of the distributor shaft. On some General Motors distributors, the rotor is a large round cap-like fitting that *must* be carefully oriented to fit. On the underside of the rotor is a square plastic nub and directly opposite is a round nub. These nubs must be set in the holes of the same shape in the top of the distributor close to the advance weights. Secure the entire assembly with the screws provided.

17. Replace the distributor cap, which is also keyed to the distributor body, and tighten the clamp screws or "J" clamps. If you have installed a new cap, check the coil high-tension lead and make sure that each of the plug wires and boots is fully seated in its proper tower. Also, be sure that all sparkplug wires are back in their looms and that all wires are dressed clear of hot metal.

REMOVE, CLEAN, AND REPLACE BACKFIRE FLAME ARRESTER

Estimated Savings: Up to $5

1. Remove the vent hoses (if used) from the flame arrester and the valve cases and clean them with a degreasing solvent.

2. Loosen and remove the screw, clamp, or bolt that holds the flame arrester on the top of the carburetor and remove the arrester.

3. Thoroughly clean the entire unit by giving it a bath in a degreasing solvent or strong detergent and water. If you use detergent, rinse in alcohol. Some garages have degreasing tanks and might wash the unit for you or allow you to use the tank for a small fee. If kerosene is used, be sure to blow the unit dry after washing. Use a soft brush to remove the dirt from between the baffles.

This task is extremely important because dirt accumulating on the baffles of the flame arrester chokes the engine, causing poor performance, excessive smoking, and excessive fuel use. Keep an eye on the backfire flame arrester's condition all the time the boat is in use, and clean it as often as necessary.

4. Replace the flame arrester on the top of the carburetor and tighten the hold-downs. Reconnect the vent hoses.

CLEAN AND LUBRICATE OUTSIDE OF CARBURETOR

Estimated Savings: $2

1. Use a degreasing spray and an old paint brush to wash the entire outside of the carburetor. An excellent aerosol spray product is available that will loosen and remove greasy dirt and any sticky residue from old gasoline.

2. Make sure that all automatic choke linkage is clean and free to move. Lubricate it with a good quality marine grease. Give the throttle linkage the same treatment. Carefully inspect engine ends of throttle cables and controls for signs of excessive wear or chafing.

REMOVE, INSPECT, OR REPLACE ALTERNATOR/PUMP DRIVE BELT

Estimated Savings: $5

1. Loosen the clamp bolt and nut on the alternator sliding bracket. Pry the alternator to loosen the drive belt.

2. Remove the drive belt and inspect it inch by inch, inside and out. Look for cracks and signs of wear. Bending the belt back

and forth, look for cracks on the inside of the belt. If replacement is indicated, consult the engine maintenance manual for size and type or take the old belt to any filling station or auro supply store where it can be measured and replaced. A good spare should *always* be carried, and the old belt might serve this purpose.

3. While the belt is off the engine, check the condition of the belt pulleys on both the alternator and the engine. Rotate the alternator pulley by hand and check for excessive play in the bearings by attempting to wiggle the shaft. Straighten any bends and file smooth any nicks that would wear out the belt.

4. Check the pump pulley and shaft bearings. Excessive shaft play in either the pump or alternator is a clear indication of imminent failure. In most cases the entire unit must be replaced, although, alternator shaft bearings sometimes can be replaced in a shop that does that kind of work. Marine alternators are extremely expensive because they are required to be explosion-proof.

5. Reinstall the belt on the pump and alternator pulleys. Press down the alternator with a stick of wood, and tighten the belt until you can depress it one-half-inch with your thumb. Then tighten the nut/bolt combination on the alternator adjusting bracket. Use care in this adjustment as overtensioning the belt will cause excessive wear of both the pump and alternator bearings. With the belt too loose, neither the pump nor the alternator will perform correctly.

Fig. 6.14   Adjust drive belt tension.

INSPECT COOLANT, HYDRAULIC AND FUEL HOSES AND CLAMPS.

Estimated Savings: Perhaps none; but great peace of mind is assured!

1. Remove and *discard* all spring-type coolant hose clamps and replace them with flat, screw-type, stainless steel hose clamps, which are now required by federal regulation.

2. Where practical, remove the coolant hose from its metal fittings and, in strong light, look for cracks and excessive stiffness, which indicates that the life has gone out of the material. Watch for chafes and burns where the hose might have been touching hot metal. The inside of the hose might be caked with dirt and deposits of salt. Consider replacing any hose that is not in good condition.

3. Inspect fuel tank filler hoses, vent line hoses, vent (overboard) fittings, and fuel line hoses (or metal tubing) from tank to engine fuel pump. Check all clamps for tightness and any evidence of weeps or leaks. Look for corroded fittings, and clean, burnish, and coat them lightly with Vaseline. If accessible, remove the vent line hose from the fuel tank and clear it by blowing out the line. Replace and tighten the hose clamp. Be especially alert to the quality and condition of any grounding wires between the filler hoses and the tanks. Clean, burnish, and tighten them as needed.

4. If your boat uses hydraulic pumps to operate various other auxiliary systems, carefully inspect all hoses, clamps, and fittings for signs of leaking and tighten or replace as necessary.

SET TIME AND DWELL [INBOARD FOUR-CYCLE ENGINES]

Estimated Savings: Up to $25

There are two methods for timing out an inboard four-cycle engine—static and dynamic.

Static Timing

No elaborate instruments and tools are required, the boat need not be in the water, and cooling water is not needed for static timing the engine. At no time during static timing is the engine started or run. The technique results in an engine timed as accurately as with the most elaborate equipment and is acceptable to all engine designers. Perhaps the only drawback is that dynamic tests of the automatic spark advance cannot be accomplished by this method.

You will require a 12-volt DC test lamp, a box-end or socket wrench to fit the distributor clamp bolt or nut at the base of the distributor and a bump switch (or jog switch). The battery must be charged and connected in the boat.

1. Loosen an remove the distributor cap fasteners so that you can view the position of the distributor cam shaft and the point set. Note: This technique assumes either that the point set and condensor have been replaced and the point set spacing has been carefully and accurately set to specifications or that the point set is OK and spaced, ready to be timed out.

2. Consult the engine maintenance manual for timing data. For example: It might say "Set time to 5° A.BTDC". This means that the sparkplug of the number one cylinder (and therefore all other cylinders) will fire *before* the piston is within 5° of cam rotation of *top dead center* (the "A" stands for *advance*). Most modern marine engines, like their automotive cousins, are set with *advanced* timing to get better performance and combustion.

3. Locate and identify the timing marks on the engine. In most cases, these are on the front of the engine. One mark is found on the idler pulley (or, as it is sometimes called, the vibration damper). This mark is often little more than a shallow groove cut in the edge of the pulley. The second mark is usually found on a small plate that is fixed to the front of the block close to where the timing mark on the damper will pass. (You may have to rotate the engine crankshaft one full turn before you find the mark on the damper.) When you have located the marks, wipe them clean with a cloth soaked in a solvent and dry them. Then, using either white typewriter correction fluid or white fingernail polish, paint a thin stripe over each mark so that they stand out better. A narrow stripe is the most accurate. Use a jog switch to bump the engine over in small increments until the two marks coincide exactly. If you have trouble aligning the marks, remove all the sparkplugs to relieve compression and turn the engine by hand, grasping the pump/alternator drive belt and

Fig. 6.15   Showing location of "typical" distributor clamp bolt.

pulling the main crankshaft and distributor camshaft into the desired position. Be certain that the timing marks coincide *before* you proceed.

4. Connect one clip of the test lamp to the engine ground and the second lead to the terminal on the coil that comes from the distributor. On the coil is usually marked "POS" ("+ or "BAT").

5. With the proper size wrench, loosen the clamp bolt or nut at the base of the distributor just enough to allow the distributor body to be turned *slightly* by hand.

6. Energize the ignition system by turning the ignition key to ON but *not* START! *Caution*: If you allow the engine to turn over, you'll have to align the timing marks all over again.

7. Carefully observe where the rubbing block on the point set is positioned on the cam. It should be very close to the high point on the cam and the point contacts should either be open or just starting to open. If the timing is way off, the rubbing block will be approaching or have gone past the high point and the point contacts will be closed. Grasp the body of the distributor with both hands and watch the lamp. Turn the distributor until the lamp *just* goes out and set the distributor body (and the rubbing block) at that point. This is the firing point for the number one sparkplug, and the points must be set to just barely open. It might take a few tries, but get it as close as you can. If possible, make an alignment mark with a pencil on the base of the distrib-

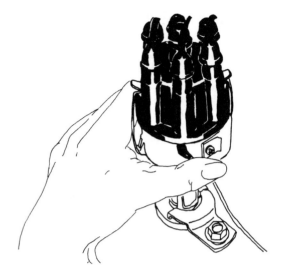

Fig. 6.16 Rotate distributor body by hand till lamp JUST goes out.

utor shaft at the point where the shaft goes into the block. This will help to maintain the alignment as you tighten the distributor clamp nut/bolt. Carefully tighten the clamp. Remove the test lamp. Turn off the ignition key. Replace and tighten the distributor cap retaining fasteners. Replace the sparkplug if you have not already done so. Your engine is now in time.

Dynamic Timing

This method of setting time and checking the cam dwell angle requires some of the special instruments mentioned in previous chapters. In addition, the boat must be in the water or supplied with cooling water by hose. The battery must be installed and normally connected. You will need a combination dwell/tachometer point resistance meter and a neon or xenon powered timing light, a wrench for loosening the distributor clamp bolt, and a medium-size screwdriver. If you have a GM distributor with a window that permits dwell setting by means of an adjustment screw, you will need an Allen wrench to fit the screw head.

1. Remove the high tension wire from the coil and connect it to a good engine ground to prevent dangerously high voltages

from either damaging the coil or giving you an unpleasant surprise.

2. Connect the black lead of the dwell meter to a good engine ground.

3. Connect the red lead of the meter to the terminal on the coil that comes from the distributor.

4. Set the dwell meter selector switch to *dwell*. (Note: this procedure may be different for other types of meters. Consult the instructions packed with the meter.)

5. Turn the ignition switch to ON but do not start engine yet.

6. Observe the reading on the scale of the dwell meter. If the reading is either 60° or 45°, set the selector switch to *point resistance test*. If the reading is 0°, the points are open and the engine must be jogged until the meter reads 65° or 45°.

7. When you have the correct dwell reading and have set the meter selector switch to point resistance, all is well if the indicator needle of the meter is within the *green* area on the bottom scale. However, if the pointer is out of the green area, there is an excessive amount of contact resistance between the faces of the point set. As in all low-voltage circuits on small craft, circuit resistance cannot be tolerated, and the condition must be corrected before you proceed.

There are two primary causes of contact resistance at the points. If the contact surfaces are excessively corroded or pitted it is best to replace the point set. If the point faces are out of alignment and do not make sufficient surface contact, the contact must be carefully and slightly bent to bring the two surfaces of the contacts into alignment. A pair of needle-nosed pliers and great patience will bring the points into alignment. When you have readjusted the points, again carry out the point resistance test with the meter until the reading is in the green area.

8. Refer to the engine maintenance manual to determine the proper amount of dwell angle required for you engine. If you do not have the manual, your dealer might be able to supply the required data.

9. Reconnect the high tension wire from the coil to the distributor. Set the selector switch of the meter to *dwell*.

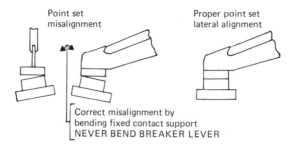

Point set misalignment

Proper point set lateral alignment

Correct misalignment by bending fixed contact support
NEVER BEND BREAKER LEVER

Fig. 6.17   Contact resistance reduction by proper alignment.

10. Note that on most meters there are two scales to read dwell angles, one for 6-cylinder engines and the other for either 4- or 8-cylinder engines. If you have and 8-cylinder engine, use the 4-cylinder scale and double the reading. Know the proper reading *before* you start the test.

11. Start and warm the engine and set the throttle for a normal idle RPM. After the engine has warmed up and the automatic choke has opened, observe the dwell reading on the proper

Fig. 6.18   Checking the dwell (point spacing) with dwell meter.

scale for the number of cylinders in your engine. Dwell settings of most engines are specified in a range of degrees. Some typical settings are: 4-cylinder engines, 31°-34°; 6-cylinder engines, 31°-34°; and 8-cylinder engines, 29°-31°. It is best to shoot for an adjustment in the center of the range. If the dwell reading is too high, the points have been set too close together and must be readjusted. If the reading is too low, the point spacing is too great and must be adjusted until the reading is within the correct range. On a GM-type distributor, this adjustment is made with the engine running, using an Allen wrench through a little sliding window on the outside of the distributor body. On other distributors, the point spacing is reset with flat feeler gauges. (This is why we emphasized setting them correctly the *first* time!)

12. When you have the dwell angle as near to the center of the specified range as you can get it, gradually increase the RPM of the engine by operating the throttle arm at the carburetor, letting the engine drop back to normal idle. Observe the dwell meter as the RPMs are increased and decreased. If your distributor has a pivoted breaker plate, a variation of as much as 12° is normal and can be ignored. However, if your distributor breaker plate is *not* the pivoted type, a variation of more than 2° or 3° indicates the possibility of a worn distributor shaft, bushing, or breaker plate, and you must turn to a professional.

Special cases   Some marine engines have dual breaker points. To test the dwell, put a piece of cardboard between the point faces of one set while you test and adjust the second set of points. Then move the cardboard to the adjusted set and test the first set. When both sets are adjusted, test both sets together with the cardboard removed. If they are in individual adjustment, the total dwell should also be within specifications.

If the distributor has an automotive vacuum advance system, the hose running to the vacuum unit must be disconnected and plugged (with a pencil or golf tee) during dwell testing.

13. Test the centrifugal advance mechanism of the distributor to be sure it is working properly. (If there is a vacuum advance system on your distributor, disable it as described in the previous paragraph.) Set the dwell/tachometer to the TACH position and idle the engine around 500 RPM. Loosen the distributor body clamp bolt/nut and turn the distributor body by hand until the maximum RPM reading can be obtained on the meter. Hold the

distributor steady at that point and increase the throttle setting to obtain a reading of 1,000 RPM. Again try to increase the engine RPMs by rotating the distributor body slightly by hand. Do not change the throttle setting during this part of the test. If the engine speed can be increased more than 100 RPM over the previous reading of 1,000, then the centrifugal advance mechanism is not working properly and must be repaired. Call the professional at this point. Naturally, this test knocks the engine completely out of time and you will have to re-time the engine to specifications as before. Do not forget to reconnect the vacuum hose to the distributor when you have finished re-timing the engine.

Continue the testing by checking out the balance of the cylinders to make sure that each cylinder is doing its share of the work. This test will further illustrate the versatility of the meter and give you the confidence that *you* know the condition of your engine before the boating season commences. This test can be used at any time to add to your data while preparing your PPM program and to locate and identify one or more of the following problems: weak or faulty cylinder pistons (i.e., compression rings); weak or faulty valves (i.e., burned valve, broken valve spring); or a faulty sparkplug (without removing them all to inspect).

It might be helpful to enter the results of this test in your Engine Use-Time Log for later analysis. Of possibly the greatest value to you, *this test is predictive*. It will warn you of a borderline cylinder that may not require immediate attention but will need corrective maintenance soon.

CYLINDER BALANCE TEST

Estimated Savings: Difficult to estimate, but considerable.

1. Gather the following tools: dwell/tachometer, insulated sparkplug wire-puller, (an old plastic fuse puller will do), clothespin ignition tester (see Chapter 2), and either a shear pin or an old bolt that will fit into the end of the sparkplug wire rubber boot.

2. Connect the dwell/tachometer to the ignition system (red lead to POS on the coil terminals and black lead to a good engine ground). Start and warm the engine to normal operating temperature and set the meter selector switch to TACH. Adjust the idle throttle for an indicated RPM of about 900.

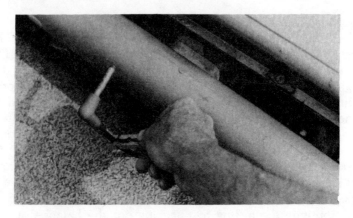

Fig. 6.19   Cylinder balance test. Ground spark plug leads one at a time.

3. Watching the tachometer reading, remove the sparkplug lead from the first cylinder (the order is not critical, as long as the are *all* done, one by one). Ground the lead by inserting either a shear pin or a bolt that will fit into the rubber boot. To avoid an unpleasant shock, use an insulated tool or wooden clothespin and stay well clear of engine metal while handling the sparkplug lead. As you ground the lead, the RPM of the engine should drop slightly. Any cylinder operating below normal efficiency will cause a less than normal RPM drop. Record the RPM drop of each cylinder in the Engine Use-Time Log. Often a significant drop in RPM can be traced to a bad plug, but as mentioned it is necessary to test the compression of the cylinders to pinpoint the cause. (See later paragraphs on compression testing.)

AIR-FUEL RATIO TEST

Estimated Savings: Possibly substantial fuel savings

1. Have at hand a dwell/tachometer and a piece of flat material such as a metal plate or sheet of cardboard.

2. Start and warm the engine to normal temperature. Set the manual throttle to give an indicated RPM of 750 on the meter.

3. Remove the backfire flame arrester from the carburetor throat and set it aside.

Fig. 6.20   Air to fuel ratio test with sliding cardboard sheet.

4. Observe the reading on the meter as you *slowly* slide the flat sheet over the air horn of the carburetor to partially block the air intake. If the RPM *increases* as you slide the sheet, the mixture is too lean in the carburetor, (too much air and not enough fuel). Conversely, if the RPM *decreases*, the mixture is too rich (too much fuel and not enough air). Oddly enough, a lean setting will cause the engine to run hot, and a rich mixture will cause the engine to run cool, resulting in excessive smoking, wasted fuel, and fouled plugs. If the RPM does not change significantly until the air horn is almost completely covered, the air-to-fuel ratio is acceptable.

5. To test the backfire flame arrester for proper function leave the engine running after the air-to-fuel ratio test has been completed and watch the RPM indicator as you reinstall the flame arrester. If there is a drop in RPM with the flame arrester in place, the unit needs cleaning.

AIR-TO-FUEL RATIO ADJUSTMENT AT CARBURETOR

Estimated Savings: Very high if fuel mixture is too rich

1. Have at hand a dwell/tachometer, a screwdriver, and your engine maintenance manual.

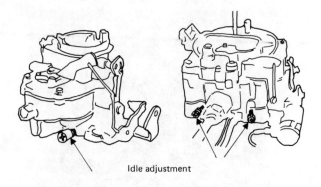

Idle adjustment

Fig. 6.21   "Typical" idle mixture adjusting screw(s) on a carburetor.

2. Determine the manufacturer's specifications of idle RPMs and adjust the idle adjust screw on the carburetor near the throttle linkage. (To locate this adjusting screw consult the manual.)

3. Locate and identify the idle mixture screw(s) on the carburetor. (These screws are normally found at the base of the carburetor and can usually be identified from the spring in back of the screw. Refer to your manual.)

4. Very slowly turn the mixture screws in either direction to obtain an *increase* in RPM. If an increase is indicated on the tachometer, readjust the idle setting of the throttle idle screw to specifications. When there are *two* screws to be adjusted (often the case on the larger V-8 engines), adjust each screw alternately, back and forth for maximum reading. This is necessary since the adjustment of one screw will often affect the setting of the other. Each time you get an increase of RPM over the specified idle speed, reset the idle throttle adjusting screw to the correct RPM. Once you have "milked" the last possible RPM from this adjustment, the air-to-fuel idle mixture should be correct.

CYLINDER COMPRESSION TEST

Estimated Savings: Could be substantial

This test can be most conveniently conducted just after the engine has been tuned up for the season. It is effective when the cylinder balance test using the dwell/tachometer has detected a

Fig. 6.22 Testing compression. Note spark plug cleverly concealed under hot manifolds.

lazy cylinder that could not be cured with the installation of a new sparkplug.

Compression testers are usually inexpensive and, like all instruments, come in a variety of styles and features. The simplest is little more than a meter with a rubber cone that is inserted in the sparkplug hole and held there manually as the engine is turned over with a jog switch. However, this type of gauge is difficult to hold against the extreme pressure generated inside the cylinder of a high-compression engine. For high-compression V-8 engines, or any engine in which the sparkplugs are hidden under manifolds and other attachments, we recommend the type of compression gauge with adapter plugs that screw into the sparkplug threads in the block and connect to the gauge with a hose.

You should make up a table listing all cylinders on your engine. Label one column "Initial Pressure" and a second column "Final Pressure." When the data from each cylinder is collected and tabulated, it can be analyzed to determine the engine's problem.

The test, while very simple to conduct, requires several carefully thought out steps.

1. Determine from your manual or dealer the specifications for normal cylinder pressure.

2. Gather the following tools and materials: a compression tester; a sparkplug wrench; a long-nosed squirt can filled with

Fig. 6.23   Prop the throttle plates and choke plates wide open. This keeps fuel out of the engine during test.

30-weight oil; and a couple of screwdrivers or small blocks of wood to prop open the throttle plate at the carburetor. While not absolutely required, a jog or bump switch, is useful. Without the bump switch, you will need an assistant to operate the starter switch at the operating station.

3. Start and warm the engine so that the engine lubrication oil is at its normal temperature. Readings on a cold engine will be false.

4. With the sparkplug wrench, loosen all the sparkplugs and *carefully* blow or brush off any accumulated dirt around the base of each plug. To avoid burned hands, use the sparkplug removing and starting tool described in Chapter 2. After you have cleaned the base of the plugs, remove and set all sparkplugs aside. As you remove each plug, put a small piece of masking tape on each plug wire with the number of the plug printed on it. This will ensure that each wire is reattached to the proper plug.

5. Remove the back-fire flame arrester from the carburetor air horn and prop the throttle plates *wide open*. Since the engine will be cranked during this test, no fuel should be drawn into the cylinders. Use the screwdrivers or little blocks of wood to hold open the throttle plates wide, which will break the vacuum in the intake manifold and prevent fuel from being drawn into the engine.

6. Remove and ground the high tension wire from the coil to the distributor end, using a clip test lead. This precaution need

Fig. 6.24   Pressure release valve at bottom of gauge.

not be taken if you are using the jog switch rather than the normal ignition switch.

7. Connect the jog switch to either the starter assist solenoid terminals or the starter solenoid terminals. Use the maintenance manual to locate and identify these points.

8. Operate the jog switch to turn the engine over several times. This will blow out any remaining dirt in the sparkplug hole threads.

9. Connect the compression meter to the first cylinder to be tested. Use the manual to keep careful note of the identification of the cylinder under test. The technique is simple but exacting. As you turn the engine over with the jog switch, catch the first reading on the gauge and then the final reading which the gauge will hold for you. The first reading, as the piston completes its first compression stroke, is important. Subsequent strokes will cause the needle of the gauge to gradually increase and stop at a maximum point. Stop turning the engine at the highest reading on the gauge. As you turn the engine there will be a loud popping sound as the pressure is released from each cylinder by the exhaust valves—don't let it bother you.

10. On the table you have prepared, record the initial reading and the final reading of each cylinder. You might have to take several readings on each cylinder to get the hang of it. Release the stored pressure from the gauge each time you take a reading. The pressure release valve is either at the base in the rubber tip or on the side of the gauge and is similar to a tire valve.

11. Analyze the data gathered from the test. Usually the engine maker specifies the *lowest* acceptable percentage reading that the test must show for each cylinder. For example, the lowest

pressure allowed might be listed as within 75 percent of the highest reading cylinder. If the highest reading cylinder is 200 pounds per square inch (PSI), then the lowest reading must be 150 PSI or more. Manufacturers list this data differently, so take the time to study and understand what *your* readings must be.

We can make some basic assumption about cylinders that did not fall within specifications. If you found two cylinders side by side in which the pressure recorded was low, you have a blown head gasket that must be replaced. If you found one cylinder that had a low reading on the first stroke and failed to build up to minimum specifications on subsequent strokes, you have one of two problems—either the valves are bad or the piston rings are at fault. To eliminate the possibility of bad piston rings, retest the cylinder in question. But first, give the cylinder a few squirts of 30-weight oil by inserting the nose of the oil can right into the sparkplug hole. Retest the compression of that cylinder and note the new readings. Compare both sets of readings. If there is a 10-pound increase, then you must conclude that the rings are worn and an expensive ring job is in order. If there isn't a significant increase, the problem can be traced to a worn, sticking, or burned valve, and the remedy is a valve job. If you found an excessively high reading on one or more cylinders, there might be a build-up of carbon deposits within the cylinder head. It is possible to confirm this by "reading" the sparkplug for that cylinder, which will show excessive oily black carbon deposits. A sticking choke, a dirty flame arrester, or an overly rich fuel mixture can cause carbon build-up. Check these possibilities before trying a higher heat range sparkplug.

REMOVE AND REPLACE FUEL LINE FILTER AT CARBURETOR

Estimated Savings: $3 to $5

Next to battery problems, fuel failures cause the greatest number of calls for assistance. And, like the battery problems, most of these failures could have been prevented by a small amount of PPM. When a boat sits idle for a long time, many problems can develop in the fuel system. Water tends to condense in fuel tanks to cause rust and corrosion of the tank and fittings and to form harmful chemical combinations. If not attended to by the PPM skipper, these problems will appear at

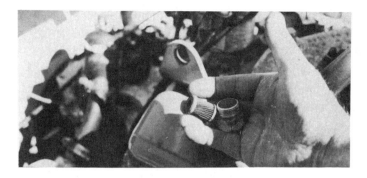

Fig. 6.25   Carburetor fuel filter (inboard engine). Filter element was distorted during removal.

the fuel filters. The filters, doing their job, collect most of the undesirables and become loaded with contaminants. As if this were not problem enough, your fuel has probably already been contaminated at the fuel dock, where the pumps, tanks, and fittings are subject to the same rust and corrosion. Periodic use of fuel additives and conditioners will go far in reducing or eliminating contaminants, but PPM of the fuel system will do more.

Many modern marine engines have a small but important fuel line filter installed close to or directly on the carburetor. This little replaceable cartridge filter should be changed at least once during the boating season. Use the engine maintenance manual to determine the part numbers of the filter cartridge, spring, and fiber washer (if used) and purchase a complete replacement set. You will need a large open-end wrench to loosen and remove the filter nut. Use a bit of Vaseline or light grease on the threads.

1. Back off the retaining nut of the fuel filter at the carburetor. This fastener must be drawn up tight to prevent fuel leaks, and sometimes the chemicals in the fuel form sticky shellac-like coatings on the threads making it difficult to disengage. Use care and patience to break that first grip of the retaining nut. A second wrench may be needed to hold and turn the filter body instead of turning the retaining nut. Take care not to damage or dent the metal fuel line.

2. Carefully remove the filter cartridge, spring and washer and examine them under a strong light. Look for signs of solid con-

taminants such as rust flakes and metallic particles. The presence of these particles indicates trouble upstream of the filter that requires immediate attention.

3. Replace the old cartridge with new parts and carefully hand-start the retainer nut. *Caution*: It is very easy to cross-thread fuel line fittings.

4. Nearby (and often part of) the fuel pump is a second fuel filter. The removable glass bowl once common in filters is now illegal and should be replaced with a metal bowl. At the base of this filter you will normally find a screw clamp which can be loosened by hand to release the filter bowl. Do not allow the bowl to fall into the bilge and spill raw gasoline. If there is a filter element, which looks like a screen cloth bag, remove it from the bowl for examination and cleaning. Empty the contents of the filter bowl into a glass container so that you can see what filter bowl has been trapping. Wash the filter element in clean alcohol and blow dry. Check the nature of contaminants removed from the bowl. Any significant amount of water will appear as a separate layer of liquid and indicates that your tanks need a couple of cans of fuel conditioner.

5. If you haven't already done so, inspect all fuel lines back to the tanks and check the condition of hold-down clamps, shut-off valves, and any ground connections on rubber fuel line hoses.

INBOARD DRIVE TRAINS

Estimated Savings: $20

1. If the lubrication oil (gear case) is reasonably fresh, check the oil level with the dipstick and top off as necessary. (*Note*: Dipsticks are often hidden under filler plugs. Check your owner's manual.) If engine use-time hours so indicate or an oil sample shows signs of deterioration, drain the old oil (see Chapter 2). Refill with fresh oil. Start and warm the engine for ten minutes, then shut it down, recheck oil level in the gear case, and top off as necessary.

2. Inspect the entire drive unit for oil leaks, rust, corrosion, and signs of excessive wear. Remove the cable connectors and check the gear shift levers for freedom of action. Check any clevis pins in the cable ends for signs of excessive wear and

Fig. 6.26 Checking shaft alignment AFTER boat has been launched. (Simulated-actual shaft not shown)

replace as indicated. Renew cotter pins and lubricate cable end connectors. Have an assistant operate the gear shift from the control station as you observe for correct length of travel of the gear shift assembly.

3. Check tightness of coupling bolts, mounting bolts, and all fasteners.

4. Grease all zerk fittings (inboard) around the shaft stuffing box. Check hoses and clamps around the shaft (if used) for condition and tightness.

5. After the boat has been in the water for several days, inspect and measure (with feeler gauges) the shaft/drive unit coupling alignment and adjust as required. This alignment is tricky, and you might be wise to call in a professional to do the job. In any event, do not attempt to do it before launching because a wooden boat will swell or take a different set when it has been in water.

6. Check the drive shaft gland nut and any stuffing box fittings for tightness. *Note:* Some systems are designed to allow a slight drip of water out of the inboard fitting, so do not overtighten.

Fig. 6.27   Checking stuffing box fittings. (simulated)

7. Before launch, recheck the condition of *all* external fittings associated with the drive train. Inspect the shaft and rudder sacrificial zincs for condition and tightness. Shake the shaft struts and check mounting bolts, strut bearings, and zincs (if used).

INBOARD/OUTBOARD DRIVE UNITS

Estimated Savings: $10

1. Inspect the entire unit for signs of rust, corrosion, and galvanic action. *Note:* Few outdrive units are *directly* protected by sacrificial zinc anodes. If you have an outdrive that does use a zinc anode as a trim rudder, and if it shows signs of pitting and erosion, replace it now. A pinhole leak in a lower gear case (the result of galvanic action) will soon give you a thousand-dollar problem. Check the condition of hydraulic shock absorbers and outdrift raise or lower power units for the same problem.

2. Pay particular attention to the stainless steel bonding strap that electrically bonds an electric shift outdrive to the engine. If there is not a good clean connection under the strap, the unit can jump out of gear at high speeds and destroy a drive shaft. Remove the hold-down bolts, burnish the surface of the metal under the strap, and reconnect the ground strap.

3. Drain and flush the upper gear case (if used) with diesel oil or number 2 fuel oil to remove traces of dirt and sludge.

4. Refill the upper gear case to proper level with recommended hypoid gear oil. Do not overfill.

Fig. 6.28 Zinc trim rudder. Note the portions eaten away by galvanic action.

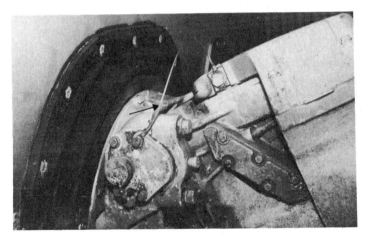

Fig. 6.29 Outdrive electric bonding strap.

5. Check the oil level in the intermediate housing and top off as required.

6. Drain and flush the lower gear case (see item 3 above) and refill.

7. Inspect the sacrificial zincs mounted on the hull under the drive unit. Replace any zinc that has been one-third consumed. Check the cleanliness of the zinc mounting bolts inside the hull where they attach to the engine block or intermediate housing.

Fig. 6.30 Sacrificial zincs on outdrive hull. Through bolts connect to intermediate housing and engine.

8. Drain, flush, and refill the gear cases (or top off the hydraulic oil reservoirs) of the powered drive unit, raise/lower systems. Provide power to the system and carefully test the unit while boat is out of the water.

9. Lubricate *all* zerk fittings on the outdrive unit with special water-resistant grease. Consult the owner's manual, which lists and describes each fitting, its location, and the type of lubricant to be used, and follow these instructions religiously. Do not overlook hidden fittings. Test the steering while the boat is out of the water.

Inspect the entire steering system from operating position to outdrive. Look for loose, rusted, and corroded fittings. Apply grease liberally to steering cable fittings.

10. Inspect the propeller, drive shaft, shear pin (if used), shaft nut (if used), and propeller hubs. Renew cotter pins. If the propeller was overhauled in the off season, it should have been *dynamically* balanced and a new shock hub fitted inside the propeller.

11. Lightly wire-brush any remaining marine growth. *Caution:* Do not paint the lower unit with an anti-fouling paint that is incompatible with the metal of the drive unit. Scratches and normal surface wear on the lower area of the drive unit expose raw metal and set up the conditions for galvanic action between the copper of the anti-fouling paint and the aluminum alloy of the drive unit. If you must paint the drive unit, use only the paint recommended by the maker of the drive unit.

Fig. 6.31   Propeller, cotter pin, hub, shear pin—inspect carefully.

12. *Never* test drive units with the engine running without supplying cooling water to the engine. Most drive units supply cooling water to the engine circulating pump by means of a lower unit pump. These pumps use a rubber impeller that is lubricated by the water flowing through them. If you run dry, a pump of this type will be useless after a few turns.

After the boat has been launched, test the output of the lower unit pump. Make sure the engine is up to operating temperature and the thermostat is fully open. Remove the hose(s) from the intermediate housing where it connects to the exhaust manifold, and discharge the output of the hose into the bilge or into a large container. Start the engine and observe the stream of water from the hose. The stream should be at least the size of the inside diameter of the hose. *Note:* If the volume of output from any hose is low, call in a professional mechanic. Shut down the engine and reconnect the hoses. Test the output of the manifold hoses the same way. Do not run the engine with a hose disconnected for more than a few seconds, just long enough to evaluate the volume of water coming from the hose.

7
OUTBOARD ENGINE PPM

The conventional two-cycle outboard engine is universally designed for the purpose of driving a boat through the water. Many inboard engines are simply converted motor vehicle power units that, unless substantially reinforced, do not withstand the marine environment as well as the outboard engine. This is especially true when the engine is operated in salt water. This does not mean that the outboard engine requires less preventive maintenance, for a well-planned PPM program will pay off in more reliable outboard performance. Preventive maintenance of an outboard is more convenient because it is more accessible than an inboard engine. Often, however, this advantage is offset by the number of special tools, jigs, and fixtures required to do some of the simplest preventive maintenance tasks on this type of engine.

In the last few years there has been a trend (especially in the larger outboards) toward extremely sophisticated electronic ignition systems. These systems are encapsulated or "potted" in a solid material that prevents disassembly for repair. They can only be replaced. Despite the impossibility of repair, the electronic ignition system represents several advantages over the older conventional systems. In new engines, for example, a higher energy spark results in more positive firing of the sparkplugs. In older engines, the lubrication oil, mixed with the fuel, often inhibited positive firing and tended to foul the plugs. Also, distributor components need not be routinely replaced in an electronic ignition system. Points no longer routinely burn because they are no longer switching heavy increments of current. Finally, starting the engine may be more positive and

Fig. 7.1   Electronic ignition components on modern outboard engine.

easier due to the characteristics of the new ignition system. Should any of these components fail, however, the components must be replaced.

The sophisticated test equipment and the advanced factory training required virtually prohibits skippers from doing even the most routine corrective maintenance and leaves little to do in the way of preventive maintenance, at least with respect to the ignition system. The reduced need for preventive maintenance almost eliminates most corrective maintenance.

TOOLS, INSTRUMENTS, AND MATERIALS FOR OUTBOARD PPM

Much the same but fewer tools are required for outboards as for inboards. Refer to Chapter 5 for suggestions regarding on-board tool boxes and shore-side maintenance lockers. A wheel or bearing puller is essential for skippers with smaller engines who expect to renew their point sets and condensers. The torque wrench suggested for inboards is also a virtual necessity. There are few instruments more useful around the outboard than the simple test lamp. While more sophisticated instruments are available, their cost and fragility do not make it practical to carry them in the tool box. A combination dwell/tachometer and timing light is just as useful on outboards as inboards for doing tune-ups. A grease gun loaded with the best quality of marine grease is an absolute requirement as are small containers of light machine oil, Vaseline, penetrating oil, and spray cans of silicone-based lubricating and insulating material such as WD40. Several containers of gear case oil (Hypoid) for the lower unit of the engine should be carried on the boat so that the gear oil can be changed or topped off during the season.

Documentation

Normally, each engine comes with an owner's manual that contains at least routine preventive maintenance requirements and schedules. This manual should be used as a basis for your PPM program. You should consider purchasing the shop manual for your engine if you are serious about doing as much of your own preventive maintenance as possible. At first you may be dismayed by the highly technical language in this manual, but remember that it was not written with the owner in mind. Confusing points usually can be cleared up by studying the illustrations along with the text. As you might expect, the shop manual is devoted mostly to corrective rather than preventive maintenance, but a few evenings of study during the off-season will pay off later in many cost savings.

Some method of recording engine use-time hours is every bit as important with outboard engines as with inboards. There is no other sensible way to determine the need for periodic preventive maintenance. If you cannot afford an electrical engine use-time meter, at least try to keep a faithful log.

On-Board Spares

In deciding what engines spares to carry on the boat, ask yourself, "What *might* fail in this engine that could be repaired *only* by the replacement of a part?" By all means carry spare sparkplugs already gapped for your engine and ready to install. Carry at least two or three spare shear pins for smaller engines. Include a spare propeller, at least one spare fuel filter element, and, if used, cotter pins, safety washers, and zinc trim tabs.

The larger engines seem to be covered with small hoses running in every direction, most of which are associated with

Fig. 7.2   Mercury outboard engine propeller washer—tabbed.

the fuel system. A length of spare hose for each system is easy to carry and could well save the day. Don't forget the proper clamps for spares.

A small can of gasket sealing compound is required for some engines, not for gaskets but for daubing on the propeller shaft splines to help keep water out of the gear case.

PRE-SEASON TUNE-UP OF OUTBOARD ENGINES

Propeller and Drive Shaft Assembly

Start at the bottom of the engine at the propeller and work your way up to the top. Remove the propeller by straightening the cotter pin or the tabbed safety washer. Special pliers for use with tabbed washers are available from engine dealer. Keep the washer but replace the cotter pin. Immobilize the propeller by wedging a piece of wood between the blades and the trim tab. Remove the propeller nut. Removing the propeller from the shaft may require the use of a wheel puller.

Carefully inspect the condition of the propeller. Pay attention to the inner rubber shock bushing (new bushings may be needed). Check the shaft splines (grooves cut in the shaft). Wash them with a solvent; lightly sand them with crocus cloth to clear up any corrosion; and apply a coating of gasket sealer. If the propeller has nicks or a bent blade, send it out to be refurbished and balanced and install the spare.

To mount the propeller, first install the large nut (if used), then the tabbed washer, and finally the smaller nut. Bend the tabs to keep the hub nuts from backing off. Tighten nuts to specifications in your owner's manual. Some engines use a

Fig. 7.3 Zinc trim tab and water intake screen.

Fig. 7.4 Water intake screen. Inspect behind the screen if possible.

simple spacer and cotter pin to do the same job. Don't forget that the spacer (large washer) goes *behind* the propeller nut. Tighten the nut, then install and bend the cotter pin.

Inspect the trim tab. On some engines the tab performs a dual function of trimming the steering and acting as a sacrificial anode to prevent damage to the lower unit from galvanic action. Consider the outright renewal of the trim tab if any significant portion has been eaten away, and give some thought to why the galvanic action is taking place—it might be preventable. Now is a good time to adjust the trim tab if it has been necessary to carry extra right or left rudder while steering.

Inspect the water intake ports and screens (if used). Make sure that these intakes are completely clear of any old marine growth, paint, or anything that might restrict the flow of cooling water to the lower unit water pump. Small barnacles can pass through the screens, attach themselves to the inner passages, and grow enough to choke off the cooling water. If the screen is removable, take it off and inspect the inner area for anything that will clog this vital passageway. A light coating with an organo-tim type of bottom anti-fouling paint will keep most marine growth out of this area in the future. *Do not* use a copper-based anti-fouling paint, for you risk galvanic action between the paint and the metal of the lower unit.

Fig. 7.5   Changing oil in lower gear case.

Drain and flush the lower gear case and note the color of the old oil. If it is the color of coffee with cream, there is water leaking into the gear case and something must be done to stop it immediately. Flush with diesel oil or number 2 fuel oil to remove any sludge or dirt. If the engine is less than five years old flushing may not be necessary. Refill with fresh Hypoid gear oil (grease) and insert and tighten first the upper fill level plug, then the lower plug. Make sure the plug gaskets are in good shape.

Inspect the entire area of the engine under the power head—tilt mechanism (if used), steering swivels, mounting brackets and bolts, reverse lock systems, steering pulleys, cables, and springs. Be especially critical of electric cables that must turn with the engine. Cables that have chafe spots underneath, where they rub on the transom, may develop troubles later. Following the owner's manual, lubricate all fittings with the proper type of lubricant.

Remove the engine shroud. Inspect and lubricate the latching mechanism and give the cover a bath in strong detergent and water. Most covers are fiberglass reinforced plastic with a gel coat finish. If the cover gel coat is showing signs of dullness, give it a rubdown with a good quality gel coat cleaning and rubbing compound, then wax and polish it with gel coat waxer.

Detach and lay aside out of the way both throttle and shift cables (assuming mechanical shifting). Starting at the outside of the shift lever, check all shifting linkage for freedom of movement and grease each swivel point with the grease specified in the owner's manual. Operate the shift lever by hand several times to work in the grease, then check again for free movement. On this last step, check the safety start switch that

Fig. 7.6   Shift cable linkage and throttle linkage.

prevents the engine from being started while in gear. As a rule this switch is linked to the shift lever. From time to time its clamp screws loosen and allow the switch to get out of alignment. Before reconnecting the shift cables, place the shift arm on the engine in the neutral position and place the shift lever control at the operator's station in the neutral position in its detent. Adjust the end of the shift cable travel to just match this position at the engine shift lever. Clean exposed metal parts on the shift cable of any rust and corrosion and coat them lightly with grease or Vaseline.

Carry out similar procedures with the throttle arm, checking the linkages up to the carburetor and spark advance mechanism (if used). Make sure all fasteners are tight but free to move with the linkage.

Check all electrical connections on the engine. First, inspect the terminal lugs. Any terminal lug showing the green patina of corrosion should be removed and burnished clean using non-conducting fine sand paper, given a light coating of Vaseline, and reconnected and tightened. Use the proper size and type of screwdriver so that you do not damage the heads. While there may be quite a few connections on a newer type engine, checking and cleaning them all now can save a lot of grief later.

The many small lengths of hose on a modern marine outboard engine are subjected to even more stress than hoses on bigger inboard engines. Now is the time to give attention to the hoses and their associated clamps, replacing as common sense dictates. If you have spring-type clamps, it might be wise to buy

Fig. 7.7 Example of safety switch for neutral start only.

Fig. 7.8 "Typical" electric terminal block. Inspect for corrosion and loose fittings.

Fig. 7.9 Hose clamp pliers.

hose clamp pliers, for little else effectively loosens or tightens them. Where you can, replace spring clamps with stainless steel screw-type clamps.

Lubricating oil is mixed with the fuel in nearly all outboard engines, and this mixture, when set and inactive for a long period of time, forms shellac-like substances in, on, and around the carburetor. Use a spray can of special carburetor cleaning compound to get off all of the dirt. Different brands of cleaning compound are used differently, so faithfully follow the directions printed on the can. Some brands recommend a few squirts directly into the carburetor air horn *after* the engine has been started and warmed. This type of product may clear up sticking choke and throttle plate problems with the least effort.

Now remove and inspect the sparkplugs. A plug that is excessively coated with black greasy carbon-like deposits indicates a problem in that cylinder—or possibly a problem with the whole engine. Improper carburetor settings, too much oil in the oil-to-fuel mixture in fuel tanks—there are several possible reasons for greasy deposits. "Reading" the plugs will give clues as to what the problem might be. While it is generally best to install a new set of sparkplugs on older engines at the beginning of the season, this does not apply to the newer engines that use surface-gap sparkplugs and/or electronic ignition. The surface-gap plug needs only to be cleaned (it does not have an adjustable gap), and these plugs used with electronic ignition need only to be cleaned and the gap checked.

Reinstall the plugs and torque them tight to specifications with a torque wrench. Sparkplug torque in outboard engines is somewhat more critical, since the engine block and the heads that the plugs screw into generally are aluminum alloy. Special care must be used in starting the plugs in their threads and torquing them up to the correct foot-pounds tightness.

If you intend to install new point sets and condensers (if your engine has one of the more accessible systems), leave the replacement of the plugs until after the new points are in. Many of the larger outboard ignition systems use a conventional automotive distributor driven electrically by the same type of coil used on the family car. If this is the case, you can change the points and condenser and set the point set gap spacing (dwell) following the procedures contained in Chapter 5 for inboard marine engines. *Note:* The electronic ignition packages for these engines have no provision for and do not require preventive maintenance. The engine with an electronic ignition system does not require point set changes as often as those that do not have this system.

Fig. 7.10   Removing flywheel to uncover point set on an outboard engine.

In engines of less than 60 horsepower, changing the point set can be difficult because the points (usually a double set) are hidden beneath the flywheel. After the shaft nut has been loosened and removed, removal of the flywheel requires the use of a wheel puller. Further, after the points have been installed and the dwell carefully set, the reinstallation of the flywheel involves torquing the shaft nut up to a specified number of foot-pounds. So, to do this job properly you must have access to both a wheel puller and a torque wrench. These special tools can often be rented or even borrowed, but if you plan to be a full-fledged PPM skipper, consider purchasing them. They have many other uses and eventually will pay for themselves.

One of the "tricks of the trade" may be needed to get the flywheel retaining nut loose from the shaft. The nut is on tight and simply turning it counterclockwise with the proper size box-end or socket wrench will turn the entire shaft of the engine. Blocking the propeller is not recommended because this places a severe strain on the shaft. As always, there is an easier way. In a professional shop the flywheel would be held with a strap wrench as the shaft nut is backed off. Since the sparkplugs were removed earlier, you have only to insert a short length of nylon line into the sparkplug hole. Use enough line to jam the piston so that it cannot come up to top dead center and allow the shaft to rotate. The nut can then be backed off without any danger of damage to the rest of the engine. Leave the line in place to tighten the nut after the points and condenser have been replaced and the dwell set.

At this point, the investment in an engine shop manual will pay off. The procedures for changing points on an outboard engine are no more complex than on a conventional engine and require little more than patience and the willingness to follow precise instructions. The balance of the tune-up should be

Fig. 7.11   "Typical" outboard fuel line filter.

completed *after* the boat has been launched or when adequate cooling water can be supplied to the engine during test and adjustment.

Since a lot of the problems on any size outboard engine seems to stem from fuel troubles, give the fuel system a thorough checkout, starting with the fuel tanks and ending at the carburetor. Excepting those boats that are equipped with permanently installed cruise tanks, most outboard engines are supplied with fuel from portable *steel* tanks. Fuel should not be left in these tanks during the off season. Gasoline has a strong affinity for water vapor, which will condense and start rust problems within the tank, and get into the engine to cause other problems. If the fuel left in the tank has been mixed with lubrication oil, it will form shellac-like substances that will stick up carburetors and valves. At the end of the season the engine should be run in the water with all fuel hoses disconnected and allowed to die out from lack of fuel. This will completely drain all fuel lines, the fuel pump, carburetor bowl, and the float chamber, thus reducing the danger of fire and the formation of unwanted substances. Completely drain the tanks at the end of the season and rinse out with a cup of denatured alcohol, which will take up any water and loosen any dirt remaining in the bottom of the tank. Empty the contents into a container so that you can see what you got (if anything). Pour a little more alcohol in the bottom of the tank, tightly cap it, and store it in a dry area. If the bottom outside edge of the tank has started to rust, consider wire-brushing, sanding, priming, and painting the tank.

The fuel tank often leaves a ring of difficult to remove rust on the deck area of the boat. Storing the tank on a tank plate made of marine plywood keeps the tank up off the deck and prevents rust stains.

Fig. 7.12 Inspect start cord for both manual and electric start.

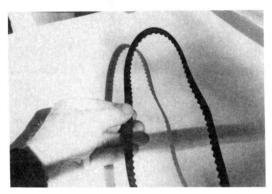

Fig. 7.13 Inspecting belt drives.

With the tanks clean and stored, inspect the fuel hoses and their fittings. They are extra tough but take a beating during the season. Make sure that the automatic sealing plugs in the ends of the hose function properly and are clear of dirt that might allow them to leak. Trace and inspect fuel lines up to the fuel filter. At the fuel filter (there is one on nearly every engine) back off the nut or screw that holds the filter element in place and remove the filter cartridge. If indicated, install a new cartridge and carefully retighten the retainer. Inspect the hose from the filter to the carburetor or fuel pump. If there is a removable bowl on either the fuel pump or carburetor, take it off and empty the contents in a glass container so that you can see what it has caught. It's a good idea to look over old filter elements and the contents of a filter bowl to see what might be going on upstream.

Give the carburetor a good outside cleaning with a spray can of solvent designed for this purpose and dry it off carefully. Lubricate the linkage on the carburetor at the points indicated in the owner's manual.

Fig. 7.14   Inspect control box electrical connections.

On an engine equipped with a manual pull start assembly, pull the cord out to its full length and inspect its condition. Replace a cord that is frayed, cut, or worn and lubricate the return spring.

This is the time to install and torque the new gapped sparkplugs. We recommend that you wait until now to do this because the engine must be turned over by hand several times during many of the previous preventive maintenance jobs.

Inspect the condition of any belt drives used on the engine. On some engines the distributor is driven with a toothed belt. On other engines the alternator may be belt-driven, although it is most often a part of the flywheel assembly. In any event, belt drives are crucial to the operation of the engine and must be in top shape. Be sure to buy a new spare for any belt that you must replace.

On larger engines that have a separate electrical control box, remove the cover and inspect all accessible connections for signs of corrosion. Burnish and coat with Vaseline before retightening them. Check the condition of the sealing gasket on the cover before you replace it.

8
STARTING A BALKY ENGINE

While not truly a part of a preventive maintenance program the material in this chapter has been included because sometimes—usually when you most want it to—even the best maintained engine will not start.

The battery, which is a chemical machine for the storage of energy, keeps on working. Acid vapors, come out of the vents and combine with air and the metal of the terminals to form non-conducting oxides. Minute stray currents leak from the terminals and follow a path of dirt and moisture, thus lowering the total charge. The automatic bilge pump draws and uses its share of battery energy. A poorly wired circuit allows a current path back to the negative terminal and leaks off more of the stored energy. While the boat is sitting idle, the alternator or generator cannot replace the lost energy in the battery. Under these circumstances it is no small wonder if a marginal battery will turn the engine over fast enough and provide ignition current at the same time!

In the carburetor, ready fuel in the float chamber may be draining back down the fuel pump line through siphoning action. The combination of gasoline and lube oil, if allowed to set long enough, forms a varnish-like substance that will fix choke plates in a position that will assure poor starting. And all the while moisture, sometimes salt, and oxygen atoms are hungrily forming new chemical combinations with every metal surface, usually where they will cause the most trouble and be the most difficult to find (in an electrical connection, for example).

In spite of all this there is one irrefutable fact. When there is air and fuel in the intake manifold, compression in the cylinders, and a spark available at the plugs, *the engine is going to start*. We need only locate and identify which of these three elements is missing and rectify it to cure the problem of a balky engine.

In almost all cases on non-starting engines, the trouble will turn out to be in the electrical system—the "soft-spot" of the internal combustion engine. The primary power source for the vital electrical energy is the boat's battery—a *low-voltage* source. Low-voltage sources must have nearly perfect low-resistance connections throughout the system in order to function. Keep in mind that a boat's electrical system is subjected to the ill effects of corrosion, electrolysis, shock, and vibration—everything conspires to keep it from working.

PROBLEMS, CAUSES, AND REMEDIES

Case No. 1

When the ignition key is turned to START nothing happens—no clicking or chattering sounds of the starter relay and no sounds from the starter motor.

Probable Causes   The main battery power switch is still set to the OFF position; the starter battery is dead and discharged; or the main starting battery cables are not connected.

Checks and Remedies   Set the main battery switch to ON and check state of the starting battery with a hydrometer. The hydrometer is the best indicator because it tests the cells one by one.Each cell should read above 1200 on the float scale of the hydrometer. Place a 12-volt test lamp directly across the battery terminals and again try to start. The lamp may glow normally at first and then dim or go out as starter key is operated. If so, battery is dead or badly discharged. Jump start with second battery and carefully watch the charging ammeter. An old or marginal battery will accept but not hold a charge. It must be replaced.

. You may follow a similar procedure using a small, low-cost, combination volt-ohm-milliammeter. Set the meter to read DC VOLTS (15 VDC or higher). Place the test leads and observe the battery (not cable) terminals for correct polarity. Operate the start key and observe the battery voltage. If it drops below 9 volts, the battery is discharged.

If the main battery power fuses or circuit-breakers are blown or open, replace or reset them and try to find the reason for the overload. Less likely (but possibly), the coil section of the starting relay may be open. Shunt a heavy jumper wire momentarily across the large terminals of the relay. If the starter motor operates the relay, the relay may be the problem. Check the wiring to the relay coil before replacing the relay.

Case No. 2

Only a clicking sound or loud chattering sound is heard when the starter key is turned to START.

Probable Causes The starting battery is in a low state of charge (see Case No. 1); and the battery terminal cable clamps and battery terminal posts are badly corroded; the battery terminal cable to the engine ground or starter relay is badly corroded; or the starter relay is faulty (use the checks listed for Case No. 1).

Checks and Remedies Loosen and remove the battery cable terminals from the battery terminal posts, and wire-brush all surfaces of the terminals. With crocus cloth, polish the contact surface inside the battery cable lugs and the battery terminals themselves. Wash off the top of the battery with a solution of baking soda and water and rinse with clean fresh water. Do not replace the cables on the battery.

Trace out the ground cable to its engine connection and give it the wire brush and crocus cloth treatment. Brush and crocus-cloth the starter or starter solenoid end of the other battery cable. When all cable ends and terminals are clean, reconnect and lightly coat them with Vaseline or grease (or spray them with one of the new electrical coating sprays). If there is another heavy cable running from the starter solenoid to the starter (or relay) clean and polish the connections.

Case No. 3

The starter motor cranks the engine at normal speed, but the engine will not start.

Possible Causes There are many possible problems either in the ignition system or in the fuel-air system. Only the most common and easily cured problems will be covered here.

Checks and Remedies First isolate the problem by checking the ignition system. To test for the presence of high-voltage ignition spark, remove the high-voltage lead from the distributor, wrap several layers of *dry* paper around the lead and hold the lead *close* to but not touching a good ground in the engine. Have someone give the engine a few turns with the starter key and watch for a bright blue spark to jump from the lead to the engine ground. If there is *no* spark, the problem is in the ignition; if there *is* a spark the problem must be in the fuel system.

If there was no spark, work back to the distributor. Connect a test lamp or voltmeter to the positive coil terminal (marked PLUS or + or BAT), turn the engine over a few times, and watch for the lamp flashes (indicating proper operation of the point set). If there are lamp flashes, a faulty coil is indicated. Install spare and off you go.

If there is no indication of voltage at the input of the coil, you'll have to check out the distributor. First, however, remove the ignition keys and put them in your pocket. Remove the distributor cap from the distributor body. Carefully inspect the inside of the cap for fine cracks, carbon tracks, dirt, or moisture. Clean it with a soft dry cloth. Remove and inspect the rotor—the spring contact and brush end should be clean and shiny. If not, clean, burnish, or, better still, replace it. Put the key back in the ignition and turn the engine over a few times as you watch the points—they should open and close as the distributor shaft rotates. If the distributor shaft does not rotate you have a problem that requires expert help.

Reassemble the distributor carefully. Dry all sparkplug wires with a dry cloth or paper towel and insulate the entire system against moisture with a silicone spray. If the problem was ignition voltage or the lack of it, you should have found it by now.

Assume that the initial spark test was positive and the problem is now isolated to the fuel-air system. Check the amount of gas in the tank(s). (Simply tap with a stick—empty tanks ring with a clear deep tone.) If you have a fuel line shut-off valve, be sure it is in the ON position. Remove the filter bowl and check for water in the gas. (Filter bowls now must be metal rather than glass.) Pour the gasoline out of the bowl into a container and allow it to settle. Excess water will drop to the bottom. If water is the problem, add a liberal portion of "dry-gas" to the tanks and rock the boat to mix it well so that it can take up the water. Replace the filter bowl and make sure that it does not leak. Try starting the engine with a little raw fresh gas poured directly into the carburetor. If there is a second fuel filter near where the fuel line from the fuel pump enters the carburetor, remove and inspect it for dirt and make sure it is clear to pass fuel. Install a new filter if you haven't done so lately. Save the dirt from a clogged filter, so its main contents can be identified. For example, rust fragments indicate you have an immediate and urgent fuel tank problem.

With the gas line and filter disconnected from the carburetor, test the fuel pump's output. Slip a plastic bottle over the end of the fuel line and crank the engine over a few times. Several good healthy spurts of gas should pour into the bottle. If not, remove and blow out the fuel line. If this does not cure the problem, then you must replace the fuel line and the filters.

Remove the flame arrester from the top of the carburetor and check the action of the choke plates by hand. Check and lubricate the automatic choke linkage—it may be frozen in one position due to heat, dirt, and salt. Inspect the backfire flame arrester. If it is dirty, it will act as a choke and may prevent the engine from starting or running easily.

If when you have done all these things the engine is still reluctant to start, it may be flooded because of all the testing and starting attempts. A flooded condition means that the cylinders and sparkplugs are wet with raw gas. The remedy is to evaporate the gasoline quickly by flushing the engine with plain air with the ignition voltage removed. To accomplish this easily, first remove and ground the high voltage ignition lead from the coil. Next, remove the backfire flame arrester and prop the choke plate(s) wide open with a screwdriver or piece of wood. Then push the throttle lever to the *wide open* position. These actions will remove the ignition voltage from the engine, brake the vacuum in the intake manifold so that no fuel can be drawn into the mixing chamber (throat) of the carburetor and admit large quantities of fresh air and nothing else into the cylinders as the engine is turned over with the starter. A five- to ten-second run on the starter motor or several short spurts should dry the inside of the engine. Reconnect the ignition, remove the choke props, replace the flame arrester, reset the throttle to the START position, and start the engine.

INDEX